CLARISSA STRACHAN'S YOUNG EVENT HORSE

CLARISSA STRACHAN'S YOUNG EVENT HORSE

Buying · Breaking · Training · Competing

DAVID & CHARLES
Newton Abbot · London

All photographs by Kit Houghton unless otherwise specified

British Library Cataloguing in Publication Data
Strachan, Clarissa
Clarissa Strachan's young event horse.
1. Eventing horses. Training
I. Title
636.1'0'888

ISBN 0-7153-9260-0

Typeset by ABM Typographics Ltd, Hull
and printed in Great Britain
by Redwood Burn Ltd, Trowbridge, Wilts
for David & Charles Publishers plc
Brunel House Newton Abbot Devon

CONTENTS

INTRODUCTION

Since riding in my first International event at Boekelo in Holland in 1971, I have competed with nineteen different horses of my own in three-day events. My horses have all been bought as youngsters, usually between four and six years old; none of them had ever competed in an event before I found them, and most were unbroken or just backed. To buy 'green' horses was originally a financial decision – unproven horses come cheaper – and I still prefer to 'make' my own horses now. Although it takes time, it is a definite advantage to know exactly how a horse has coped with previous problems when it comes to assessing his probable reaction to new questions in competition.

I was very lucky to be born the youngest child of keen horse people. My mother hunted regularly, my father rode in point-to-points and together they farmed a dairy herd on our own land at Cullompton in Devon, where we still live today. Although my brother never rode, my sister Sally was horse mad, and I followed six years behind her. Our parents never pushed but always gave us tremendous support, and at the age of five I began to ride around the farm, led by my mother. At ten I began my competitive career with a marvellous pony called Playmate. He bucked like a bronco, and learning how not to fall off and to cope properly with him was my first real lesson in producing horses. Buoyant followed – a great pony, but a true water hater – and then Dunameir, a crazy but quite brilliant Connemara, who taught me what riding something that really jumps is all about. We showjumped a little at the big county shows and Hickstead, and with her I was a member of the East Devon Hunt branch of the Pony Club event team from the age of twelve to sixteen. By then I had been well and truly bitten by the eventing bug.

Sally was eventing seriously by the time my first horse came on the scene and had passed her British Horse Society Instructor's exam with flying colours, so when I grew up enough to stop arguing and start listening I already had a first-rate instructor of my own at home. With savings of my own I bought my second horse, and from then on I have always sold a few along the line to keep the supply going: my parents had pointed out the folly of keeping *all* the horses until they were older. Producing nice

Delphy Dazzle at the National Championships at Gatcombe – all we riders were very apprehensive about these nasty-looking drops, but to my relief Dazzle worked out the problems involved and made them feel very easy!

young horses and selling some on enabled both Sally and me to expand and compete more all the time. By combining this with teaching and taking liveries for breaking and schooling Sally had developed a thriving business, and when I left school I joined her. By George! was the first horse I upgraded to Intermediate and Sally and my parents sent us both to Dick Stillwell, a terrific teacher to whom I went on frequent three-day visits with two or three horses for the next eight years. With Sally at home and at every event, and Dick to pass on all the knowledge I could soak up, I could not have had a better start to my competitive career.

During this time I learnt a tremendous amount about different horses. Both our parents had a wonderful 'eye' for picking a horse, and Sally had already learnt to spot a good one by the time I started travelling with her to buy my own. She and I are very lucky to have inherited and developed this ability – as with any other job, you cannot work with bad material. Living in Devon has been a great bonus; the South West still produces horses of a great type, and most of my 'superstars' have been found in our part of the world.

Sally married and emigrated in 1973, and since then my parents have retired and sold their excellent Friesian dairy herd. Nearly all the farm buildings have been filled with horses – at any one time I have between six and eight of my own but combined with liveries, who are constantly changing, my four working pupils, headgirl and myself are generally working a total of nearly twenty horses. My parents used to organise a BHS event at home and the cross-country course for this has now become the Exeter and District Riding Club hunter trial, so we have all types and sizes of solid fence to school over whenever we need. The self-feed silage barn has been turned into an indoor school, so our facilities are excellent and with a constant flow of young horses I never seem to stop learning all the time.

Our year starts with the older horses coming back into work in January, and they begin schooling and competing at jumping shows in February. The first one-day event comes in March, after which there are one- and three-day events virtually every week until late October. Throughout these months the older horses take up a lot of time, but I also manage to fit in some work with the new ones and youngsters – as well as with pupils and their own horses – in fact, every day there seems to be all ages and standards to work on. From October to January I usually find time to look out for and buy one or two new hopes, and I try to have them ready for a few small shows and hunter trials during the winter months.

Through constant trial and error, as well as our share of disasters and occasional triumphs, I believe I have arrived at a very workable method of producing the event horse, and I hope that some of my experiences and

Dazzle again, showing an excellent jump into water. He is obviously totally confident about landing in the pond and is very correct in his style – he is looking on towards the fence leaving the water. He has jumped far enough out to make the drop look easy but has by no means over-jumped, and is coming through well behind although slightly checking himself for the anticipated drag of the water. When the older horses do it right like this it makes all the time and training involved along the way feel so worthwhile.

guidelines can help others to do the same. I have had some great horses who have taken me competing all over Britain and around the world and given me an enormous amount of pleasure, and I have come to the conclusion that eventing is a terrific sport, addictive at every level and with every horse, from the moment you buy him to the day you compete at the big event.

The colour photographs in this book, which show my current and past horses in action, illustrate how marvellous the event horse can be when he has learnt to trust himself, his rider and the jumps they have to tackle in competition – and what a thrill it is when he makes these big, problem fences feel quite easy.

1 · BUYING

The first step on the long road to a three-day event is to find your horse, and what a difficult job it is to pick out the superstar amongst the thousands that are for sale. It would be marvellous to be able to breed my own horses, or buy them as foals, but to do this would mean keeping a large number of youngsters and/or mares in the pipeline – and financially that, for me, is not a viable proposition. I have always bought my horses as untried youngsters, but have only once bought a horse younger than four years old. This was Delphy Dazzle – the exception that proves the rule – who I bought as a three-year-old and rode to a team gold medal in the World Championships seven years later. Normally, however, the time involved in waiting until a two- or three-year-old does or does not make the grade deters me. I have occasionally bought six- or seven-year-olds who have already started their competitive careers, but again finance is the deterrent: if a horse is showing exceptional talent, he certainly won't be cheap. There is also an enormous advantage in producing your own horses from square one in that one knows how they have reacted throughout their training and career to new tasks and problems, and this is a great help when it comes to a real question in later days. My age bracket when going shopping for a potential event horse therefore tends to be between four and six years old.

Where to Look

So, where do we start? The first step is to keep your eyes and ears permanently open, and always try to keep enough money on one side in case an exceptional young horse happens to come your way. One of my nicest five-year-olds at the moment originally came to us as a three-year-old for breaking. When his owner decided to sell him, he was sent back to us for schooling on and eventual sale, but I liked him so much that I bought him myself after only three days. However, it is not usually that easy.

If I am looking seriously the first thing I do is telephone people I already know in the horse business who may either have or know of any horses of the right type that are for sale. Do not be afraid of contacting dealers; as with the private seller, some are certainly more honest than others – but at least the dealer, if you choose a good one, will have a reputation to maintain.

Next read the 'Horses for Sale' section in the local papers and in *Horse and Hound*, and always try to keep the day that the paper or magazine comes out free so that you can leap into the car and be the first to see the ones that sound good. If a horse really is the right type – and, of course, the right price – it is usually snapped up pretty quickly; conversely, when a horse has lingered after being advertised I find myself wondering why. I also advertise myself – 'Wanted, potential event horse' – in the local paper, and several of my young horses have been found in that way.

When answering advertisements or talking to sellers on the telephone I do not have a list of standard questions to ask. I try to find out how the horse is bred, what it has done, how it moves, what 'type' it is and what its temperament is like. Unfortunately, it does pay to have a suspicious mind, and you should always try to listen to what you have *not* been told: 'He's very keen' (runs away or won't settle); 'Hasn't seen much heavy traffic' (traffic shy); 'Super horse show jumping and cross country' (doesn't do dressage); the list goes on. Often my suspicions are totally unfounded and the horse looks, and is, better than expected. Equally, the owners are all different. Some people describe their goose as the world's most desirable swan whereas others are convinced that no one will like their horse and tend to make him sound awful, so unless you discover a terrible snag during your preliminary enquiries the only real answer is to go and have a look.

The other obvious way of purchasing a horse is to go to a sale. I am not a devotee of this method as the horses offered at sales for ex-racehorses, where you might expect to find a potential eventer, often have problems. Not many horses have made the grade as event horses after racing, perhaps because they have been introduced to a way of going that can be hard to alter, and of course they have often done a large amount of work at an early age which does not augur well for their future soundness. On top of this, the real event horse type would probably have been snapped up prior to the sale anyway, for 'chasing, point-to-point or even eventing. There are a few sales trying to build up a reputation for selling young competition horses, but my main objection as a buyer is again that the super-looking potential star will be out of my price bracket – good news ultimately for those in the business of breeding our horses, but not so good for my pocket.

The Ideal Horse

Let's consider our aim. In fact, we are looking for the horse who will do everything. He must move well and perform an excellent dressage test, remaining sane, obedient and sensible when super fit (nowadays a leading score in the dressage is essential to succeed at every level). He must be brave and fast with great ability, capable of going anywhere, willing and keen to do so sensibly and quickly, and have great staying power. He should ultimately be tough enough to come out again when tired, and be sound and fit enough to jump carefully and accurately. He should be capable of producing top class performances for many years. A tall order.

An ideal stamp of event horse. A good thinker, who oozes bravery in his calm outlook – somehow, though, there is a look of possible fun and games lurking there. He has a super set on neck, so should come onto the bit easily, and looks to be of thoroughbred type, with a lovely shoulder and good strong limbs. Rather a long second thigh behind, but powerful-looking hocks – a great type.

Himself, Delphy Dazzle. A 16.3hh Galeopsis offspring out of an Arthur Sullivan mare, he is one-sixteenth Dartmoor pony and as clever as a cat. A very naughty young horse, he loved to cause trouble when he could, although never about jumping. Now older and wiser, the explosions are not so frequent, although his brain is not quite as it could be for the dressage! A lovely mover and a true athlete, Dazzle has always been 100 per cent sound and fit over nine years of eventing. I wish I could find more like him.

I must confess here to having a preference for geldings. I know there have been a few exceptional mares – Claus Erhorn's Fair Lady springs to mind – but by and large there have been very few mares who compete at top level, and even fewer who stay there for any length of time. It is a tough job, and mares do not seem able to take the mental pressure of repeated fitness build-ups over a period of years so easily – probably they are too clever and realise it is a mug's game! Mares seem to have far more delicate temperaments than geldings, and consequently are more tricky to produce in the right frame of mind.

Mares can also be a problem when it comes to selling. I have always had to sell on a certain number of my horses along the way – partly to finance my competing with a few at top level, and partly because it is essential to keep a team of horses of *all* ages and standards – so the temptation to keep every horse has to be resisted or my string of super young horses will eventually become a team of geriatrics, with no prospect of selling one or two to finance buying young horses again. When I go horse hunting, therefore, I always have in mind that although I am looking for top class horses for myself I am also looking for horses who will be easy to sell on well – and, sadly, mares are not so easy to place. Of course, as the demand for competition horses increases and the geldings get harder to find, we are bound to see more mares competing and therefore a larger percentage at the top. This can only be good news, as at the end of their competitive life they will hopefully be used to breed the next generation of event horses – and a proven performer as dam must be a bonus. So, I am afraid that I do tend to talk and write about my event horse as 'he', though I am well aware that a 'she' can be just as worthy a contender for eventing laurels.

Breeding

Breeding is important when looking for a potential event horse. Look back at the history of the breed of horse you consider. Was he bred to be brave and work alone? Or did he evolve as a team horse? The event horse has to want to get out there and 'go where no horse has gone before'. He must be super brave, keen and enthusiastic, and yet sensible enough to still think and react quickly and safely. The best horses always have an almost nosey and curious attitude – they really do want and need to look around every corner and discover things. The successful thoroughbred has this attitude, and has been carefully bred to develop it. He *wants* to win and be first, and will keep trying forever to be number one – this is true event horse mentality.

The thoroughbred is, of course, a true galloping machine, and nowadays the top three-day event horse has to gallop as well as a top steeplechaser *and* stay the distance. Some slower horses do succeed by being clever and nippy, cutting corners and wasting the minimum of time, but a horse who cannot gallop will never really make the grade. He will become tired and disillusioned, start to make mistakes and eventually lose his confidence. But if galloping is easy, all the horse's talent can go into concentrating on the fence.

Thoroughbreds do, however, have a reputation for being 'hotter' and more excitable than other horses, although this may not always be justified. They are often more sensitive, but there are many who behave as sensibly as you could ever want – and some common horses who are really crazy. Temperament is desperately important in any breeding, but if you have an excitable thoroughbred horse he will probably also be *quicker* in his evasions than the heavier type and this will make him far more difficult to cope with. Any horse who is truly successful has to be sensible, and if you observe the great thoroughbred racehorses they are nearly always as quiet and 'laid back' as any other top performer.

The most usual breeding for a top event horse is either thoroughbred or 7/8ths thoroughbred, with 1/8th 'ordinary' horse. Some threequarter-breds have been top performers, but as the standard rises the need for speed increases, and the horse with less quality finds it harder. So what is the ideal '1/8th'? Look again at the long-term history. Personally, I love a little pony breeding. The native ponies have given a lot of international superstars their cleverness – my Delphy Dazzle has a small amount of Dartmoor pony breeding and I am sure a lot of his ability to make quick decisions comes from this. Ponies, after all, have looked after themselves in the wild, and their young charges when ridden, for generations – and all we riders like to be taken care of!

Looking to the horse blood, I like horses who have been used for 'brave' jobs themselves. The Irish Draught has been bred to work the fields (long, hard days), take the whole family shopping or to church and yet also to go hunting with the local hounds – even more versatile than the three-day event horse. I like breeding that has evolved for these sorts of jobs, working *alone* sensibly and enthusiastically with the stamina to do long hours. Horses who have been bred as team workers, carriage horses for example, are not the best to use – you cannot wait for your friends to go with you into the lake at Badminton. A lot of the heavier breeds were also the war horses of Europe, and that sort of heart and bravery has to be useful in our job.

Look also at the terrain the horses have evolved in. The Arab, although he can be comfortable and mannered to ride and have the endurance to cover enormous distances, has not had to cope with ditches, water drops and banks, and seldom takes to cross country happily. Equally, many of the world's best dressage horses and show jumpers are 'warm blood' horses. They have been as carefully bred and produced as the thoroughbred for this with marvellous results, and many are fantastic horses, but they do not seen to have either the staying power or speed to gallop across country. The Dutch warm blood and the Selle Francais horses do look more like real event horses, and probably as they are bred to thoroughbreds we will begin to see more eventing superstars with 1/8th of this breeding.

A very good looking horse, with one of the best and most expressive faces I have ever seen – he had half sold himself to me at the first look. He does not look capable of being unkind, and seems very inquisitive. His head is well set on to an excellently developed neck, which could make him strong. He has correct angles in shoulder and front leg, and good bone. Nice and deep through the chest, and correct length of back. Strong quarters, standing a little 'cow hocked' – maybe not quite such a good back leg as his front, but still a super stamp of horse. He looks pretty fit and very well, and although not quite thoroughbred should easily have enough quality about him to be a three-day event horse. He stands, deceptively, 17hh.

This is Halloween Time, by Right Flare out of a half Irish Draught mare. His character is exactly as his face says: he upgraded to Intermediate in his first year of eventing and is starting his international career already. He cannot resist going around every new corner, which makes him super-brave across country, and (as I suspected) his only problem is that he can use his neck to pull. He is a good mover, and uses himself extremely well when jumping – which, by all the rules, his body says he should.

My basic rule, then, is to look for thoroughbred or near thoroughbred horses, and I do try to stick to it: although I have looked at, and sometimes bought, horses with unknown breeding, the thoroughbred type is what I am looking for.

It is always interesting to know which stallion a young horse is by – but it is not a vital question to me. I am keen to see a young horse by a sire with a good record of producing performers – and sometimes reluctant to go and look at one by a father of known awkward customers – but it is always worth remembering that stallions have a lot of offspring, and just *one* superstar can make a reputation. When I went to see Merry Sovereign as a five-year-old we were warned that his sire Galeopsis (by Grey Sovereign) produced funny temperaments, and to beware. Sovereign looked right, we bought him and within two years he was a top international horse – and Galeopsis became 'the well known sire of top horses'. Delphy Dazzle was another Galeopsis offspring, but I bought him because again I liked him, not for his breeding alone.

A proven performer as dam is a definite asset, although often it is impossible to find out anything about a young horse's mother. One of my toughest horses at the moment is Master Fiddler – his dam hunted for twelve consecutive seasons before producing him, and her hardness seems to have bred true. I am not overkeen on full brothers or sisters to stars; as with people, brothers and sisters often have widely differing talents and abilities.

A fabulous, wise head. This horse shows tremendous intelligence, yet appears to be calmly thinking and considering life. A good, kind eye, with the look of a sense of humour – 1 would not be surprised by a quick explosion of high spirits. Big, pricked ears which make him look alert and honest, and head well set on to his neck – 'on the bit' should come very easily to this horse.

This is Merry Sovereign, and no horse could prove himself braver – or more of a character. He is, and always was, a law unto himself; the kindest horse you could find but the naughtiest when he wanted. His energy and enthusiasm were limitless – after ten years at International level he retired still going strong. I bought him on sight, virtually unbroken and almost unhandleable, because to me he looked as if he should sail through the final day of Badminton – which he was to do six times. He always had a natural head carriage and easy acceptance of the bit, and although he was strong he was always ridden in just a German snaffle and drop noseband, with no real necessity for a martingale.

His breeding is seven-eighths thoroughbred, by the HIS thoroughbred stallion Galeopsis, who was by the famous Grey Sovereign. His dam was by Blue Duster, by Blue Peter: the non- thoroughbred eighth is unknown, but from his size – a strong 16.2hh – I should imagine probably good old cart horse!

An interesting head. At first glance this horse could definitely be described as having a pretty head, with his almost 'dished' face, but somehow that prettiness does not give him the nervous or timid appearance that it might. His whole expression is of alert but calm interest; he has a lovely wise eye and expression, and sharp, keen-looking ears. He strikes me as a very intelligent, aristocratic and brave horse.

This is Friday Fayre, a 17hh gelding by Quality Fair out of a mare from a proven family of event horses – Lucinda Green's ill-fated Wideawake (who won Badminton) was a relative. He is almost thoroughbred and does have a tendency to get over-excited, but he is as brave as a lion and will go anywhere. A very classy horse who has started his three-day event career and is now Intermediate grade.

Wearing his winter woolies. A good example of an eye with white pigment, which at first glance seems rather mean. Yet this fellow has an interested, inquisitive look, and does not appear unkind or ungenerous. I think he would be brave and, although possibly quite a character, would try to please.

This is Nobby, a little chap who is a permanent part of our team and often shows the babies the way. He likes to have a buck and a play, but is bold and willing and enjoys his cross-country and jumping, although he has seldom competed as he is needed here.

Conformation

When you arrive at a yard the first thing to do is to stand back and take a long, hard look at the horse. I like a bold, honest-looking face. The use of the word 'face' is quite deliberate, as all the equine stars I have known have had faces as expressive as any human. He must look brave, and not too pretty. The job he has to do is a tough one; look at any human athlete involved in a risk sport and you may find good looking faces, but not pretty ones. Too small a head can often belong to a rather precious person, and I would prefer a plain, slightly larger one. The eye should look bold and honest and, as with a straightforward person, the horse should meet your eye and not look shifty. Again, the eyes should not be too close together, and the ears should be of good size and pricked alertly. I have no objection to a 'roman' nose, or white on the face – or even a white pigmented eye. Two of my best-ever horses, Radjel and Stormy Down, both had one white eye (each quite fierce-looking from the wrong side) but the normal eye was as brave as a lion on both horses.

The space under the jaw should not be too small and restricted: a head that is very narrow here can produce a horse who finds it very difficult to drop his head and come on the bit – as can a very developed underside to the neck – and a hollow natural way of going is very difficult to alter. The way the head is carried and joins the neck is also very important, and a horse with a 'well set on' head and a good neck will be far easier to train and ride. The neck wants to be of good length and well developed on top (*not* below, which tells you he carries his head like a giraffe), although often a young horse who looks very weak in the neck will develop later on.

The shoulder should have a good slope of about 45°. Too upright a shoulder will not belong to a good free mover and the horse will jar into the ground when he gallops, whereas a horse with a good shoulder will make you feel that you are sitting in just the right place as he powers along beneath you. A broad chest is necessary for plenty of engine (heart) room, and again the horse will move in a restricted way if his front legs are too close together. On the other hand, an exaggeratedly broad chest can produce rather a laboured way of moving. The withers should be high enough to carry a saddle comfortably behind them, though not so high as to make the rider feel that he is about to fall off over the tail, and a nice deep, round barrel below will allow for good heart and lung room.

The back should be neither too short or, worse, too long. Exceptionally short-coupled horses can be limited in their scope and gallop stride cross country, but too long a back will give even more problems. An over-long horse will always find shortening himself up difficult, and as courses become more technical all the time the ability of the horse to collect him-

A thoroughbred type who looks immature and unfurnished as yet, but with good clean limbs and a nice body. Could be a little deeper, and stronger in the second thigh, but should mature and strengthen up a lot. His neck could also be stronger, but it is set on well and he looks a horse who will be comfortable to ride.

This is Aramis, a three-year-old thoroughbred who will go into training for racing next year. A nice young horse, who definitely moves and jumps well enough to be an event horse. He is a small 16hh now, but should mature to at least 16.1hh.

PAGES 24-5

A good, chunky, tough-looking horse with a fairly plain hunter-type head. Rather small ears, but they are pricked intelligently and he looks interested in what is going on. Appears tough, brave and sensible, with a kind eye. Very short coupled and deep, my only criticism of him as an event horse is that his neck is rather short, athough it is set on well. However, his shoulder is good, and he looks as if the rider would sit in the right place.

This is Master Fiddler, a proven hard customer who thrives on the job of three-day eventing. He is tough, brave, totally honest and does not play the fool – a real cross-country horse. He finds all three phases easy, and when he gets moving his excellent shoulder compensates for the short neck – which has taken a while to 'grow longer' for the dressage.

Fiddler is nearly thoroughbred, by Master Spiritus out of a mare by Two Fiddlers who hunted for twelve consecutive seasons. He stands 16.2hh.

self easily, and to shorten and lengthen without trouble becomes more and more essential. Remember, we are trying to spot a true athlete.

The hind quarters are the real engine of the horse, and must give the impression of a well muscled powerhouse. They must stand on top of a pair of strong, functional hind legs, with the quarters and hind leg in line. A hind leg either trailing behind the quarters or appearing to be tucked in under the body will not work well and provide maximum power, and will also be subject to more strain than a correctly positioned leg. Look for a good, strong second thigh with 'clean' – not puffy – hocks, plenty of bone below that and then again good, clean fetlocks. The joints should not appear too round, as if they are they do seem to be more prone to strains, and soundness – and the potential to remain sound for many years of hard work – is what we are looking for.

The pastern should be set at an angle of about 45°, as should the foot. Too upright a pastern and/or boxy feet will indicate a tendency to 'go into the ground' and produce a short, jarring action – no good for really extravagant movement, which we need for all the flatwork and jumping, and yet again a potential source of unsoundness with jar-induced injuries. The foot should look a good shape, and as if it will keep a shoe on easily. A healthy-looking frog which touches the ground will again help to lessen jar, but if the horse is unbroken and unshod some of this can be hard to tell. Still, look for a good shape.

The front legs are even more important. The forearm should look strong, as with the second thigh, and the knees clean, as with the hocks. Then below that, tendons: the most likely part of the horse to be a source of potential grief. As the standard of competition at every level gets higher we all go faster, and more and more racing-type injuries occur.

(above right) Quite good type and body, but the limbs let this horse down. The front legs are almost back at the knee, and are pinched below it – not good for standing up to galloping. The joints show wear and tear already, which is worrying in a young horse who has not yet done any real work.

This is a four-year-old 16.1hh mare who is just broken. She would not be my choice as an event horse with her limbs as they are at present, but she is a good type and perhaps the lumps and bumps will disappear.

(right) Too chunky a type to be a top three-day event horse, but a good stamp for a novice eventer. A little upright in front, she would probably not really 'move' and have a super action. Slightly long in the back and a rather 'left behind' back leg, but she still looks an athletic horse although obviously not thoroughbred.

This is Penny, a 16hh mare who has taken her owner/rider Shirley Lewis into BHS eventing for the first time. Because she has not too much quality and speed she has been an ideal first event horse, which is what her type suggests.

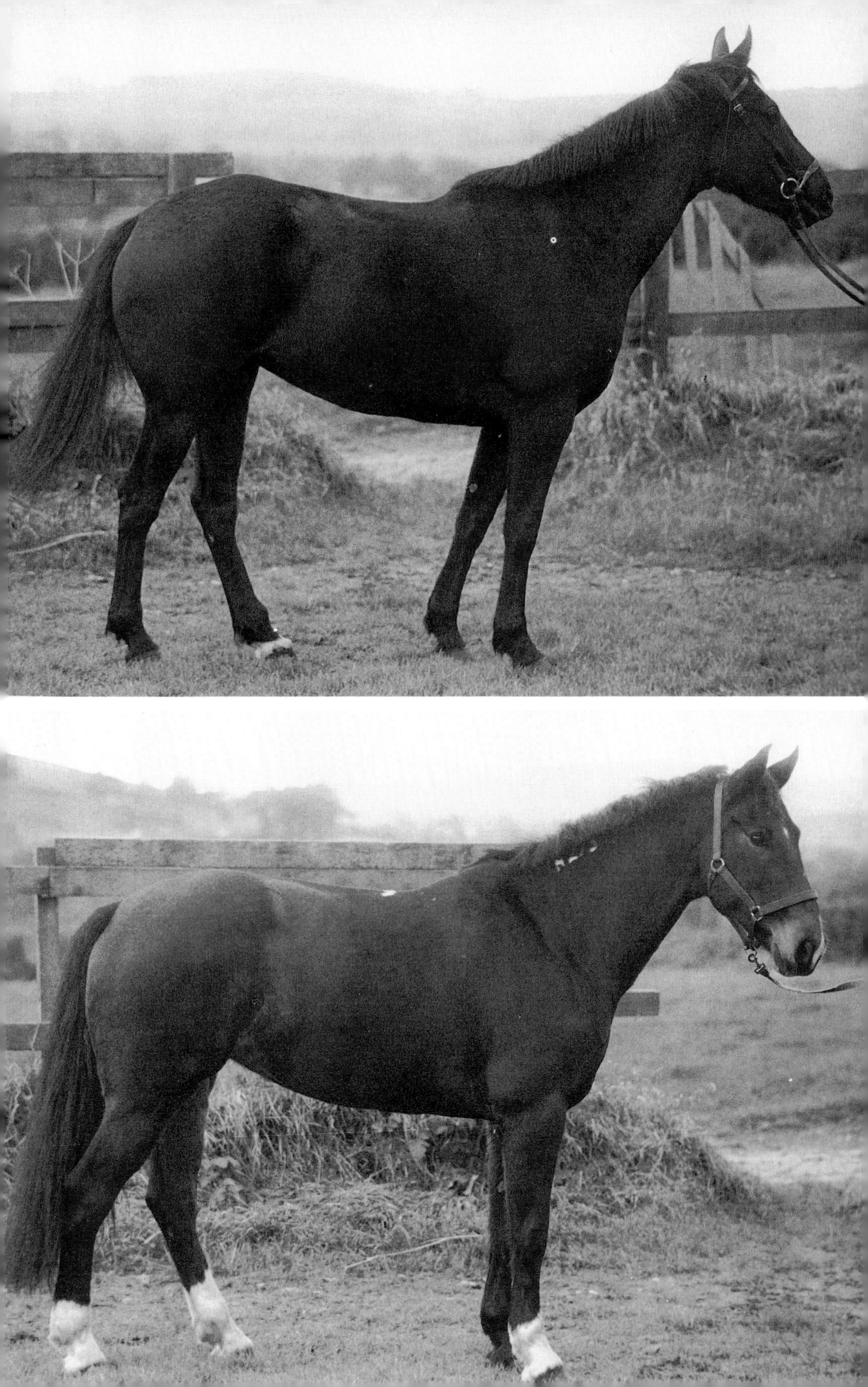

Tendon trouble is big trouble, and the need to buy horses with legs that are correct here is paramount. *However* super everything else looks, the temptation to buy a horse with doubtful-looking front legs must always be resisted. The cannon bone/tendon length should not be too long, and should be consistent in size – legs which appear to be narrower or 'pinched' below the knee are not good. Viewed from the side the leg here should look broad and strong, and from the front narrow and full of quality – flat bone, not round, is what we are looking for, and tiny little legs are not going to stand up to the job. We want clean, strong-looking tendons: they should resemble steel cables and show absolutely no sign of injury in the way of swelling or lumps and bumps. A splint in this area would not worry me unduly, providing that it was well forward and not too high. A position where any interference with the tendons or knee seemed to be occurring would be cause for concern.

As with the back leg, look again for a good pastern and foot. A long, sloping pastern will put undue strain onto the tendon, and the foot and pastern should be at the same angle as the shoulder to produce an athletic, free-moving horse.

Movement

Having decided what you think of the horse's type and conformation, now watch him walk and trot up and decide if your preliminary assessment was correct. I never tire of looking at horses and playing the game of 'would I buy that or not?'. At shows and events, and when we are training other people's horses at home, I love to make a judgement on how they will move and jump and then see if I am right. I am convinced that every fault a horse has can be spotted by looking at his conformation, but learning to spot them is the difficult part. Of course, the degree to which each little snag will affect the horse is another question entirely – the perfect horse (or, for that matter, the perfect human) has not yet been discovered.

So we bring the horse out and see him stand in front of us. How does he stand? The real event horse should stand proudly and have immediate 'presence' – you should feel he is saying 'Look at me'. The horse should not behave stupidly or in a nervous fashion; instead, he should look as if he wants to get on and do his job, but not as if he is about to charge off alone. Next, watch the horse walk away from you, then turn and walk back towards you and straight on past. This is to see whether he moves 'straight' or not; when his legs come forward they should swing in a straight line and not noticeably to one side in a 'dishing' action. Dressage judges can mark down such action, and if it is very pronounced it can put strain on the joints involved. Personally I do not mind a slight tendency to 'dish' – Merry

Sovereign always did this a little with his near fore, and it certainly never hampered him.

Now have the horse walk straight past you so that you can observe his length of stride and his action. You want to see a good swinging step, covering a lot of ground with a loose, free style. Too much knee action is not a good thing; it tends to use up a lot of effort in not really going anywhere. At walk the horse should noticeably 'track up' – in fact, he should 'overtrack' as much as possible. It is very easy to spot this by watching where the front foot meets the ground, and then observing how far over this place the back foot falls. Walk is the pointer to how the horse will eventually gallop: a horse with a good walk is invariably a horse who gallops well, while a bad, choppy walker nearly always has a similar gallop.

Having seen him walk up and back, you now want to see the horse trot in hand. Again, look for a good, straight action and floating stride. You are hoping to see a horse who is going to score a natural eight or nine one day for his trot in dressage, and who will also sail through the trot-up in a three-day event. He should have elevation in his trot stride and, as in the walk, should cover a lot of ground by engaging his hind quarters naturally and using his body.

Under Saddle

If the horse has so far shown me no awful defects or snags, and he is rideable, then go on to see him ridden. Incidentally, if you have already decided no at this stage it is not *always* so easy to get away. I have never forgotten an occasion many years ago when I went on a horse-hunting expedition with my sister. We had a lot of horses to see, and quite early in the day came upon a chestnut threequarter-bred horse. Although he was probably too heavy, we both felt that if he really moved superbly he could be possible, and so we asked to see him walk and trot up. He was led down the road, turned and started to trot. We could see immediately that his action was not good enough, conferred quickly and turned to make our polite excuses and move off to the next stop. The horse was still trotting, fast, with its owner rapidly losing control with every stride. She finally let go, and he disappeared down the road at a gallop towards the local golf course. Leaving became impossible, so we joined in the chase, regretting we had ever asked to see the horse outside. After about an hour of following enormous hoof prints across virtually every green on the golf course, and evading understandably irate golfers, we finally found him happily grazing, thankfully unhurt, and carried on with our travels.

I have learnt over the years to try to see the horse ridden before I get on him – some people seem to think that a prospective purchaser may be just the person to climb aboard their young horse for the first time. Luckily not too many owners play tricks like that, but it has happened, and I would far rather see what I am about to try to ride. Watch very carefully *how* the rider gets on. Are they given a leg up or do they use the stirrup? I learnt this lesson the hard way one day in Cornwall. My parents and I were looking at a very nice little black horse. Having liked him in the stable and in hand I asked to see him ridden. I paid no attention to the owner getting on, and liked what I saw of him ridden. Then came my turn to ride him, so I put my foot in the stirrup, started to swing up and off he went. No one had yet mounted him from the ground using the stirrup and the poor little horse had the fright of his life. After clinging to his side for about a hundred yards of fast, panic-stricken leaps I realised I was never going to get astride him, lost my balance and shot off backwards into six inches of liquid, muddy field. Without change of clothes in the car, I had to look the most dreadful sight for the rest of our day's horse-hunting. Luckily neither I nor the horse were damaged, and in fact when I was legged up onto him by the most apologetic owners – who had never thought what might happen – he made no objections to me again. (Incidentally I did not buy him, but falling off before even getting on was not the reason.)

Apart from the safety angle of not riding a horse before watching him under saddle, this is another opportunity to see how he carries himself and his rider. Do you still think the same of his action and character? And does the rider look as if he is sitting and being carried comfortably and in the right place on the horse? I like to see that 'star quality' look as he is ridden around, although at times in muddy fields in Devon and Cornwall with a one in two slope everywhere it can be quite a feat for the horse to move at all. I have even, on occasion, had to decide whether to buy or leave alone with only a road to ride along.

Under saddle you can see the horse canter for the first time. A good canter is essential for a jumper, and an event horse certainly has to be that. Yet again he should have a good, athletic, elevated stride. It should look effortless and comfortable to sit on. Eventually the horse will need to be able to shorten and lengthen his stride instantaneously, and now is the time to try to assess whether his natural canter stride will make that easy or not. The ability to alter the canter stride naturally is one of the greatest attributes of the real cross-country horse – my Delphy Dazzle is by far the most brilliant, natural cross-country person I have ridden, and he has always had the ability to double or halve the length of his stride and make it feel effortless. Watching the canter should give you the impression of a controlled powerhouse, and it should look as if jumping will be a piece of cake. If the horse is ready, see him move on and gallop if possible. He should look businesslike and really get on with it – my sister always used to say a horse should look as if he would not be disgraced in the local point-to-point – and his stride should open out and cover the ground, not look as if he is driving down into it. It is a great bonus if he stays calm after galloping, too – a horse who settles easily is a great advantage.

Riding the Horse

If all is still well, now is the time to ride the horse yourself. Generally by this stage your mind should be fairly well made up. If you have already decided he is not the horse for you, then politely thank his owners and do not ride him. When selling a horse I am always grateful if a buyer is brave enough to say 'Thank you, but he is not quite what I am looking for' and does not ride my horse if he has already decided not to buy. Every different rider, however good they may be, is a new problem for a young horse to adjust to, and why give him unnecessary problems?

Once you get on board yourself you are really making sure that the assessment you made of the horse from the ground was correct. Does he feel comfortable and athletic, and is he easy and willing to ride? I do like to feel that the horse is nice in the mouth. This is a very difficult thing to describe, particularly when a horse is very young and/or unschooled, but still, over the years and through many horses, I have consistently found that a horse who has real 'mouth problems' – one who sets his jaw and either has no reaction to attempts to steer or brake, or deliberately evades the aids, or one who is very fussy and inconsistent in the contact he takes – tends always to be a problem. In dressage and on the flat it can often be improved considerably, if not entirely cured, but when it comes to galloping fast over fences the old problem tends to re-emerge and time is wasted at every event tactfully getting the horse back under control. A horse who feels as if he is happy with a bit in his mouth, and is willing to accept and obey the commands, will be a lot easier to cope with. I also like the horse to go forward freely and easily. It is important when buying to recognise what type of horse you yourself like and ride best – and I know I am lazy about using my legs and like a forward going horse.

Jumping

Having ridden the horse on the flat, and if you still like him, the next step is to see him jump. Once again, the horse's attitude is terribly important, for in the future he will have to be brave yet sensible, and that is what you want to see now. He should look where he is going and *think*, and yet at the same time be obviously enjoying himself. Do not worry if he bucks and has fun, but if he rushes and charges as if to get it over with quickly this

A tiny fence, but what a good, extravagant jump. The horse is looking at what he is doing, and looks keen but sensible (almost rather studious). Good use of head and neck in the air, and excellent 'snapping up' of knees and forelegs. He is engaging his hind legs and quarters well, and although the picture is a little early you can see that his back is already rounding into the classic bascule. Buy a horse who jumps like this when he is a baby, and then all you have to do is train him to jump this way always *(Bob Merrifield)*.

is certainly cause for concern. If it is possible to see him jump a spooky fence or even a cross-country jump (a ditch is ideal) all the better, or you could even ask to see him go through a stream or some water. If he is a really brave horse he should appear to relish the more interesting jumps; if he stops and shows real reluctance at any fence it puts a very large question mark over his boldness, particularly when it is at home over his own fences. Watch carefully for any sign of 'nappiness' – most green horses will hang a little towards home but try to spot the one who would love to go home *now*, and is prepared to have a battle if given half a chance.

The attitude is half the jumping, the style is the other half. Not only does our modern event horse have to be a careful and accurate show-jumper, but he also has to cope with increasingly technical fences across country. To do this well he has to jump in a correct style, with a round scopey jump and with the centre of his 'bascule' over the centre of the fence. I like to see a fairly exaggerated jump – though not laboured and full of effort – as I have found that as keen horses learn to gallop and jump fast later on they tend to flatten out their natural style only too easily, and a horse who could always be a showjumper as well as a cross-country horse is a great bonus. This ability to jump round and correctly also makes coping with cross-country problems such as coffins, banks and combinations very much easier. The size of the jumps that the horse is currently jumping is not terribly important at this stage. Generally I am looking at very green horses who are only jumping tiny fences, but even if the horse is further on and has done much more I am after a feeling and look of real scope more than proof of him jumping a certain height.

When you get on to jump the horse yourself you should feel immediately that you *want* to jump him. As with the flat work, he should be fairly willing to listen to your commands and let himself be ridden: the horse who ultimately is easy to ride into a big fence on a good stride usually feels equally easy going in to 'meet a fence' in his very earliest days. He should feel fun and keen to jump, and the effort involved should be nothing at all. In fact, when a horse feels right you should not want to get off him – and then you will know that this is the one to buy.

The Final Decision

One final little test remains. If possible, ride back to the stables and then either ride straight past, or turn and ride quietly away again. This can be particularly useful when you have limited facilities for trying out a horse, or a very green horse who cannot do too much, as it can just show you if he has a dubious character. Only too often the awkward or nappy customer will take strong exception to going away from his comfortable stable again, and a really difficult character is not the one to buy.

Having decided to go ahead and buy, I always say 'yes' subject to a veterinary examination. However perfect and ideal the horse may be, however much you may *know* he is the next Olympic gold medallist, if he is not one hundred per cent sound he will never make the grade. It can be heartbreaking when your vet says all is not well, but that is why he examines him – to make sure you are not buying a problem. With every stage of buying the maxim is 'Never buy a problem', and the veterinary side is no exception. Lumps and bumps, old scars and minor notes do not matter if the vet is happy he will do the job, but at this stage it is his advice to buy or not that you must follow. And if all is well, away we go to collect the new star. We have an old pony here, and either he or Merry Sovereign is called into action as nanny to collect the new boy – and bring him back to start his new career as my young event horse.

2 · BREAKING

The Right Age

Breaking in is one of the most important phases of a horse's education. 'What is the ideal age for breaking?' is a question that is often asked – and one that must receive a 'depends on' answer. For an event horse three is really the very earliest age to start. Up until then a young horse should be left alone to develop by himself. His health should be monitored carefully, with a regular worming programme and good food, and he should be looked over every day – too many lovely horses have been badly blemished by wounds that have been noticed in the field only when it is far too late to stitch or treat them properly.

Young horses do not need to be over-handled. If they are halter broken and taught to be confident with people at an early age it makes life far easier when they are older and stronger, but they must not be over-fussed and fiddled with until they become like large dogs. Some keen owners will do this, and the result is horribly pushy and over-confident three-, or four-year-olds who have no respect and are not at all easy to break. Horses develop the best characters if they can run free in interesting fields with their friends.

The advantage of breaking at three is that the horse has not yet reached his full strength or awareness of his capabilities, and should therefore be easier to cope with. The one problem is that at this age he will have to be turned away again quite quickly as he will be too young to do a lot of work, and if he proves to be slightly tricky a difficult dilemma could arise: do you keep him in work until you are quite happy he is established in *your* way of going, and risk putting 'too many miles on his clock' too soon, or do you turn him away not going quite as you like and know he may be more difficult next year?

The four-year-old, of course, will be far more mature – as well as bigger and stronger. Coping with him could be a more difficult job, but at least when he is backed he can be taken right on, even to the stage of early competitions. Still, if I had a young horse from an unbroken three-year-old I would ideally take time to break him in at three, and then turn him away again and re-back him at four. Here at home we often have horses that we have broken returning to be re-backed the following year, and we usually find that they have not forgotten their lessons and come back very quickly to the stage they were at before. One thing is very important — once the breaking process starts you should carry on until the young horse is hacking out quietly both alone and in company. He should also be quite happy to be mounted and dismounted without help from the ground, and be able to cope with fields and quiet roads. Then he is ready to go home, carry on, or go back out in the field. I do prefer to break in my horses in the drier months in the summer, as it is so nice to be able to ride them on in the field without getting into trouble for leaving enormous footprints everywhere!

Loose Schooling

So into the stable they come. We are lucky enough to have a small indoor school in which to work the horses (previously it was a self-feed silage barn for my father's dairy herd), and before this we had a fenced-off sand area outside. In my opinion some sort of an enclosed school is absolutely essential for breaking – I certainly would not want to try to do the job without.

The first time we take a young horse to the school we try to have at least two of us there, and preferably three. We let him run around loose with only a head collar on and have a good look at everything in the school by himself. When he has settled and seen all the horrors, we then quietly get him to 'loose school' around the outside of the arena. It is far easier to encourage a young horse to go forward around you without the restrictions of a lunge line at first, and if he does try to turn around it should be possible to anticipate this and move quickly behind him and keep him going. It does seem to be easier to teach youngsters to lunge when they have first mastered the basic principle of moving forwards by themselves while loose schooling.

Handling

Every day the horses are groomed and their feet are picked up. Some youngsters have never been handled at all, and so this is not always very easy. Tie the horse up in the stable, using headcollar and rope, to a small piece of string and just take it slowly. Sometimes it is necessary to have an extra person to hold him at first, and it is essential to be patient. A horse who has never really been touched is bound to object to a nasty stiff brush on his coat, so to start with just talk to him and use your hands. If he is really shy, be content with handling as much of him as he is happy with, and every day confidently go a little further. Right from day one I am firm – really naughty tricks like kicking or biting must not be tolerated. A good slap with the hand, or even with a short whip for really bad misdemeanours will show displeasure; if he panics, however, we must go back a stage and build up to repeat the exercise. Firmness and confidence will quickly win the day.

Picking the feet up is very much the same. Start with the front feet, hold them up for a while and tap them, then try the hinds. If the horse objects, go back to the front feet and then try the hind again. We have an area where our blacksmith shoes all the horses, and I like to make sure the 'babies' are happy to stand in there and allow anyone to pick up their feet and tap them before we first put shoes on. To get a youngster totally confident with grooming and picking up his feet is very important, and can be a quick job or a slow one – but it always takes patience and time. This process goes along hand in hand with the lungeing and exercise programme, and I love seeing how unhandled youngsters gradually turn into real ridden horses.

Lungeing and Long-reining

We usually start lungeing on the second day. Again it is a great help to have three people, so that two can be a presence outside the circle to stop any attemps to charge off. At first all we want is for the youngster to learn the basic commands and to walk and trot freely on both reins. I like to teach youngsters to canter on the lunge, largely to reduce the risk of bucking when they first canter with a rider – canter strike-off is always a favourite time for bucks and it is nice to know that an explosion is *not* on its way with a rider. Cantering on a small circle is not at all easy for a green horse, and it does not matter if he only manages a few strides: it is the strike-off that we want to see happen in a settled, easy way. Once the youngster is going freely on both reins on the lunge, it is time to start introducing tack – and often time for the fireworks to begin.

We do all of our pre-backing schooling and saddling work on the lunge and in the stable. I do not generally long-rein my youngster and have yet to be convinced that I should. I like to be able to *see* how they are carrying themselves and feel that with our methods (plus the great advantage of an indoor school) the end result is certainly good enough for me. There are many systems of achieving the same end product all the way along the line to the established advanced horse, but the most important thing is to stick to a basic pattern of work that proves successful.

First Tack

The Roller

The first tack that we use is a roller. The horse is installed in as safe a stable as possible – one with a high roof (bucks can be horribly high, and it is alarming how often young horses cut their heads throwing themselves around however careful you are) and a top door. Again three people are necessary: one outside to hold the door closed (and be ready to open it to let us out), one to hold the horse, and the trainer. I use a headcollar with the rope just threaded through the noseband rather than fastened, so that it can be released easily and quickly with no sudden jerk or movement.

First we show the horse the roller, let him sniff it and realise what it is. It is important to keep talking to him all the time to keep him concentrating, then we rub it up and down his neck and shoulder and gradually bring it back onto his back from the right side. Never, ever be tempted to hurry this job – when a young horse does decide to panic or fight the first restriction he has had around his body it is not funny, and is one of the most potentially dangerous situations you can have with horses. To be trapped at the back of a stable with a bucking bronco in it could be lethal, and an awful lot of youngsters do buck like rodeo horses when they first feel a roller, so all the time we have the roller on the horse's back I make sure that both I and the holder are between the horse and the door, ready for a quick exit!

The next step is to take the roller and touch the horse's stomach and legs with it before letting it hang from his back, to make sure that if it swings and touches him he is expecting it. We then put the pad on top of his back and place the roller in position under his stomach. Do this slowly at first, then gradually do it a little faster and put a little pressure on it. When the horse is quite happy with this and standing quietly without tension, then we remove the roller and change over to the left side. Everything now has to be re-positioned so that we can still eventually make our getaway. Repeat the procedure, and then gradually lower the long end of the roller over the horse's back. Now it has to be taken under the stomach, which can cause problems. Take it very slowly, trying not to suddenly pull it tight, and gradually draw the two ends together. It is important *not* to be tempted to do the buckles up too soon; I like to take my time and carefully, by stages, put as much pressure on the two ends as there will be when they are fastened. Now for the tricky bit – to get the straps firmly buckled before letting the horse go. Carefully put the straps through, but do not put the buckle pin in and, while talking to the horse, make sure that the holder is ready to release him. Fasten the buckles quietly and quickly, and move carefully backwards with the holder to the door, telling the horse to stand.

Once we are safely out of the door we must encourage him to move. Quite a few youngsters walk about fairly quietly, but most tense and jump when they first feel the roller as they turn – and some are spectacular. Shut the top door, ideally a mesh or barred door that can be seen through; otherwise stay by the door and wait until the horse has settled. We then leave him for several hours before lungeing as usual. Sometimes a youngster will buck when he feels the roller around him when he is outside, but usually the worst bucking fits have already happened in the stable. I am always very careful to be out of range in case I get kicked outside; and always use a holder when I remove the roller for the first time, taking it *very* slowly again as I do so.

The Bridle

The same procedure is repeated each day until the horse is quite quiet and confident as the roller is put on, and is lungeing normally. I like eventually to have the roller girthed tightly in preparation for the saddle, and so tighten it carefully as we go along. I usually start to introduce the horse to a bridle during this stage, just a plain rubber snaffle, with a loose drop noseband to discourage any real opening of the mouth. This is initially put on in the stable, and then left on while the horse is lunged. The lungeing cavesson is fitted on top of the bridle, and no reins or side reins are used at this stage. With a horse who is headshy I never object to dismantling the bridle, slipping it over his neck and then creeping it forward into position gradually. Taken quietly like this, the headshy ones gradually become confident with the bridle, and with time will allow you to put it on normally – and a fight has been avoided. It is best to have as few battles as possible; they are inevitable at times, but should be few and far between – and once started *must* be won.

The Saddle

When the youngster is happy with his roller, it is on to a saddle. We have a marvellous old saddle we use for this stage. It has no stirrup bars left and must be a product of decades ago, but it has good safe girth straps and is quite indispensable – I think it is probably worth a few pence, but to us it is invaluable. The first time we put it on we follow exactly the same procedure as with the roller. Most youngsters are very interested in sniffing and examining this strange thing, and it is important to remember that it is a fairly large object and will make a noise when it flaps about when they finally move. It is terribly important to make sure before letting the horse go at first that the girth is tight enough not to allow the saddle to slip over – the horror of a saddle under the tummy could terrify a young horse for life. The first time he moves in the stable, and the large dead-looking object moves too, the horse may put in a bucking effort again, and I am always very aware that as he comes outside for the first time and really begins to move explosions could be imminent. Generally, though, if the roller stage is well established the saddle bucks, if they happen, are fairly short-lived.

Reins and Stirrups

Once the horse is going happily again with the saddle we can add reins to the bridle and just let them run back under the saddle flap when he is in the

HALLOWEEN TIME: The usual Hal expression of 100 per cent interest and love of his job

CROFT ORIGINAL
68

MASTER FIDDLER: (left) Here at the National Championships at Gatcombe, Fiddler is jumping a corner fast and well, and is allowing me to turn him in the air very easily, ready for the next fence

DELPHY DAZZLE: (above) a good example of how to jump into a coffin fence. Dazzle has obviously been pulling quite strongly on the approach, but has jumped very cleanly and, although at this moment he is braking hard for the short distance between rails and ditch, he is quite clearly totally committed to jumping on out. Typical Dazzle

MERRY SOVEREIGN: Aged fourteen, he had jumped this drop fence at Downlands several times before – and decided to do this ridiculous great leap for fun. In his day Sovereign was one of the great characters of the sport, and I am sure his immense enthusiasm was the reason for his long and successful career school and working, to create a 'long rein' amount of contact. I sometimes use no further side reins than this, as many young horses – particularly those with correct conformation – will begin to drop down onto the bit and carry themselves on this contact. With a horse who is unhappy and/or fussy with his mouth I will use a loose side rein, and on occasion have used one in the stable, but I tend to play this one by look and feel. When the horse is happy with his flappy saddle and rein, we can add the stirrups and let them hang down while he works.

As soon as the horse is confident with a saddle we can begin to handle it while we are with him – usually in the school before starting lungeing, when we stop to change the rein and again when we finish. Stand next to him, each side in turn, and tap and bang the saddle, raise the flaps and let them fall. Reach over to the far side, leaning against him, and flap that side. If he panics it doesn't matter – just start again. A rider will be far more noisy eventually.

Backing

Once the horse is lungeing with all the tack on and is quite happy with the flappy saddle it is time to start leaning on him. I am not a believer in 'dumb jockeys' – sacks or stuffed trousers tied onto the saddle. They are surely far more terrifying than a human who has proved that he is kind yet firm and can be trusted, and I am worried by the thought of what could happen should a dumb jockey begin to slip. There are many ways to the finished product, but mine is straight on to leaning.

We have a small yard within our main stable yard which is about thirty feet long by fifteen across. It is bordered by the stable buildings on three sides and a gate on the other, and is the area where we wash or groom the horses outside. It has proved amazingly useful for doing all our early leaning work – perhaps the horses feel reassured by being right in the centre of the yard. There is, of course, no inclination to rush off back to their box – they are there already – and the other horses behaving in a normal way in their stables seem to exert a very calming influence. The size is also ideal: it is large enough for several people and a horse, yet not large enough for the horse to escape from his handlers.

We start by just hanging on the side of the saddle, which *must* have previously been girthed up firmly when the horse was being lunged. A helper holds the horse while the rider just hangs from the saddle, both sides in turn. A third person is then needed to give the rider a leg up. Not all the way up though: just half way up the saddle, while the helper still takes most of the rider's weight himself. Each time we do this we gradually raise the rider higher, and let the horse take more of the weight, until the

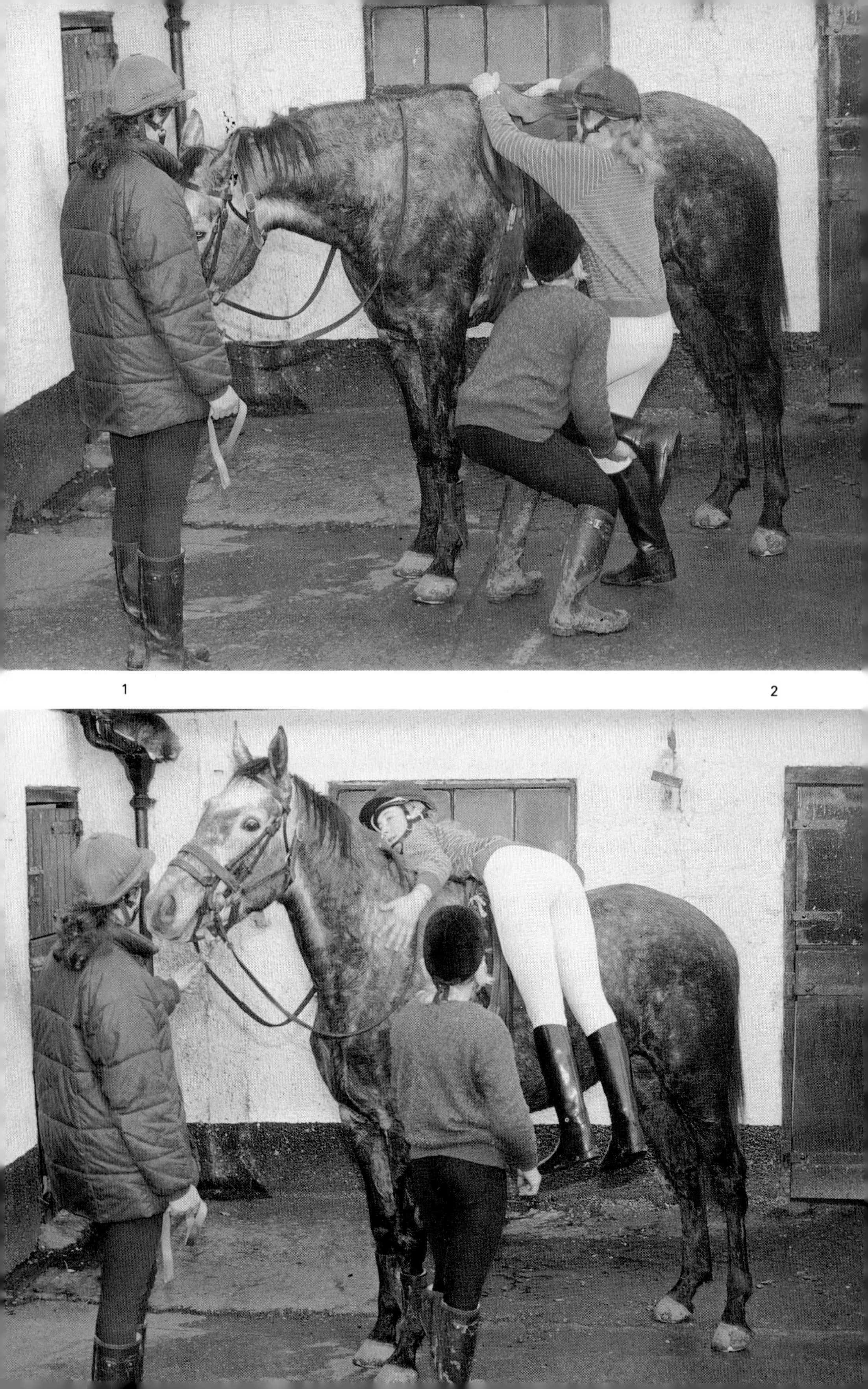

1

2

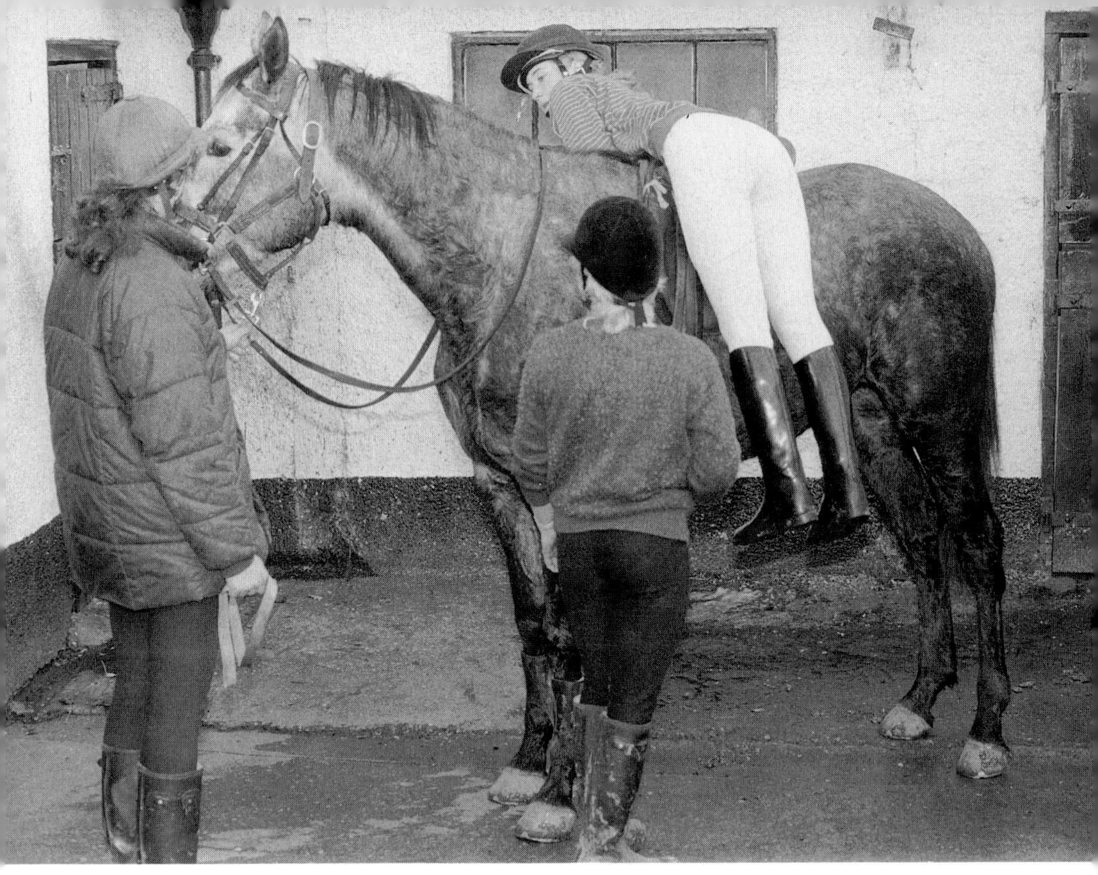

3

Leaning After hanging on the saddle, we come to our first leaning lesson. The rider is given a leg up (1) and the horse, Dodger, is not quite sure what she is doing (2) but as she talks to him quietly he relaxes (3).

rider is actually leaning across the saddle. We do this from both sides, to ensure that our horse is quite happy about 'things' hanging down each side – just as the rider's legs eventually will be. Now we have to move him. Just push him over, so he only really shifts his balance but still feels the extra weight. If this causes no concern, then we encourage him to move just one or two steps forward. At this stage if there is any panic the rider can just slip off to the ground and we start again. This is plenty for the first day, and back to bed he goes.

Every day now we try a little more leaning, working on the horse after his lungeing until he will walk around the little yard in both directions with the rider leaning on either side. I do like to make sure we have brakes, so we only go about ten yards each time, stop and carry on. Corners should be taken slowly at first, as he can see the rider and feel her far more on the turn. When he is happy with this the rider can start to move around a little, wiggling her legs and raising her body as high as possible and patting him as we go – carefully at first, and then gradually introducing more and more movement.

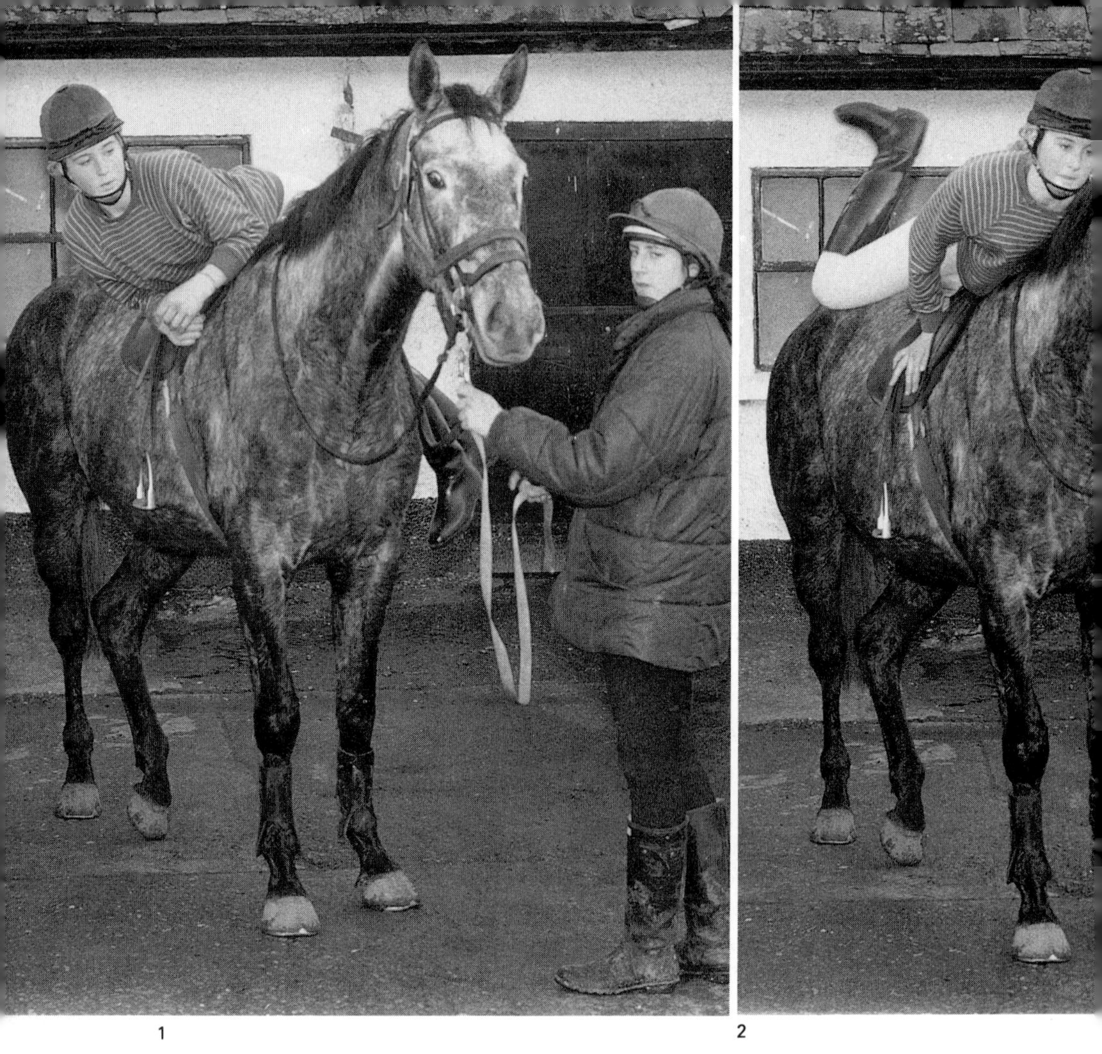

1 2

It is important at every stage not to be too afraid of frightening your young horse – a ridden horse must not be afraid of sudden movements and gradually must be taught that this is not alarming. However careful we are we will certainly move one day in an unexpected way when we are riding him – and we do not want him to panic at *that* stage!

The next movement I like to do is a swing right over the youngster's back and off the other side. This makes him realise that the rider can suddenly appear from above on the other side, just as she will when she finally mounts properly. An agile rider is needed, but then this is really essential for breaking anyway. If this causes no hassle and he seems relaxed and ready, we can start to actually ride him astride. To do this, leg the rider up to lean as usual on the left side and walk a few paces. The rider then carefully wriggles herself a little higher, and then brings her right leg up and over the horse's quarters (taking great care *not* to kick him on the way) and down into normal position on the right side. All the time she stays lying down along his neck with her head to one side. We then slowly

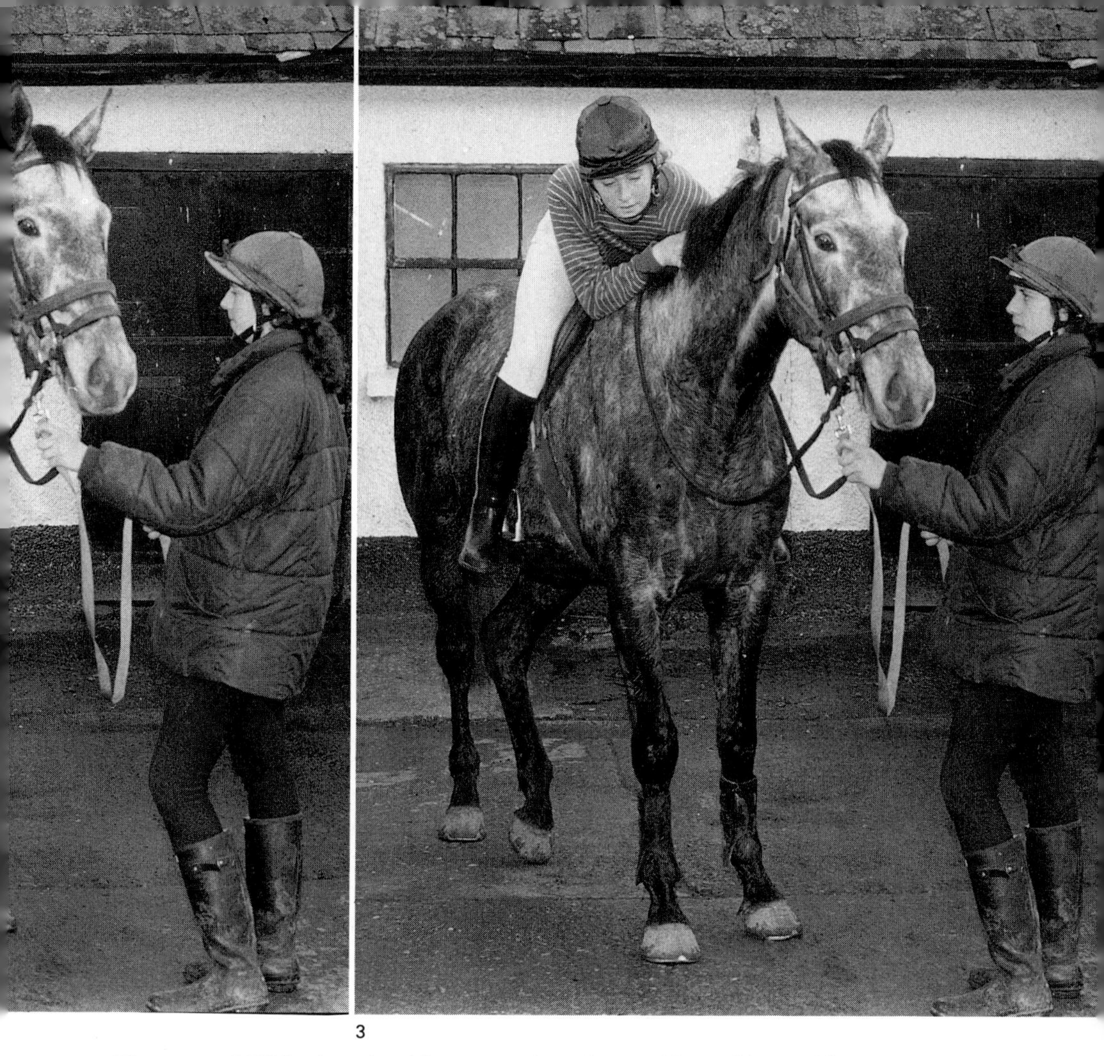

3

First steps (1)This time the rider moves into the astride position, taking care not to touch the horse's quarters as she swings her leg over (2), and still lying down on his neck and reassuring him all is well (3).

move forward and gradually get the horse moving as before. Day by day the rider sits up more, talking to him all the time.

Once the horse is happy to walk around in our little yard complete with rider we have to start making him realise that she is now in command. I like to stay in our confined space for this, and only move to the larger area of the school when my horse is obeying the basic 'stop, start, left, right' commands in the yard. Very gently and slowly, and in unison with the person leading the horse, the rider starts to introduce leg and rein aids while using her voice. Gradually the emphasis changes from leader in command to rider, and once the horse is happily obeying the rider we carefully lead him, with rider still on board, up to the school.

1

2

Once Dodger is confident with a rider sitting up (1), our holder begins, step by step, to lead him forward (2). The next stage is for the horse to take just a few steps by himself, both away from (3) and back to his holder (4).

3

4

Going Solo

Walk

I do not like to lunge a horse at this stage with a rider on top. Having once had a young horse rush off at this point, and having heard many similar tales of woe, I am loath to risk it. My disaster happened many years ago, when I was on the end of a lunge line which touched the horse on the quarters as he tried to turn and rush away. After three circuits of the school with me flat out on the end of the line behind a frantic horse (and even more frantic rider) I let go – he pulled the rein between his legs and immediately turned into a bucking machine who ejected his jockey fairly smartly. Luckily neither horse nor rider was hurt, but never again.

Instead, we *pretend* to lunge. The holder leads the horse around their normal lungeing circle, and I stand in the centre with lungeing whip exactly as if I were attached to a lunge rein. The rider gives her leg and rein aids, quietly at first and in unison with my commands, and when the horse is quite relaxed and going forward quietly, then the holder lets go of him and walks along beside him. Gradually the holder moves back into the centre of the circle to stand beside me, and the horse is being ridden alone. Still I am in command with my voice and whip, and the rider is still using her aids with me. It is very important at this stage that the rider keeps talking to the horse so he does not forget she is there – we do not want him to suddenly notice that he has a horrible thing on top of him!

Trot

When we come to trot for the first time I sometimes use my extra person to lead the horse, and sometimes not. One horse will be happier and more relaxed with someone beside him, and another will be more nervous – as with so many aspects of training horses, only experience and feel can tell you what to do. Whether we use a leader or not the idea is to try to hurry the horse in walk until he breaks into trot ‘by mistake’. Immediately, trainer and rider bring him back to walk, so he has actually trotted without really realising. Any upwards transition of pace can be alarming, as the rider feels different again, and abrupt transitions should be avoided. Next time around the circle we repeat this exercise, and allow a few paces of trot. The rider should sit quietly in sitting trot and try to be as still as possible. Each time round we encourage the horse to trot a little further until he is trotting the whole circuit. Very carefully, the rider starts to rise to the trot, keeping slightly behind the movement (safer in bad moments) and then he really is trotting properly. Back to walk, then we change the rein and do it all again. When he is trotting happily around the circle on both reins, that is enough for the first lesson.

On the next day we want to go large around the whole school, We repeat the previous day's exercise, and then come back to walk and walk going large. I walk beside the horse, still in command at about the same distance away as I was on the lunge. Second time round we trot on, and I run along beside, as quietly as possible, to keep him out. When he is going forward again around the whole school, we walk and once more change the rein and do it all again. We still lunge daily to start with, and during each day's riding we change the emphasis a little more from me being in charge in the centre of the school, to the rider. We also begin to introduce twenty metre circles at each end to start to develop more control.

CANTER

After two or three days of trotting happily we tackle the canter. We canter first just on the long side of the school away from home, and then only a few strides, using the same method of hurrying the horse as we did for trot and cantering 'by mistake', followed again by trot. The actual canter strike off can frighten a young horse into a buck, whereas introduced quietly like this it is only the same as it has been on the lunge and will usually cause no great problem. When the horse is happy breaking into canter then we keep going down the whole long side before coming back to trot, and then next time try to keep going all the way round. Even with a horse who is very free in trot and does not really need me in the centre, I find I usually have to return to jogging around on the inside and taking over command again at first in canter. When our youngster is confidently cantering around on both reins, it is time to start riding outside.

Mounting

At about this stage we have to start to think about introducing mounting from the ground using the stirrup. Only experience can tell when each horse is ready for this – the ones who were nervous about the rider leaning initially are best left longer than the unconcerned ones. When we feel the horse is ready we can tackle this after exercise when he is tired. Again, use someone on the ground to hold the horse, while the rider stands on an upturned rubber bucket beside him. (Providing time is taken to show the horse that the bucket is a safe object, it does help to have a 'mounting block' like this at first, especially if the horse is quite big – otherwise it can be only too easy for the rider to dig her foot into the horse's ribs or pull the saddle over roughly, both of which are potentially more alarming than the presence of the bucket!) Carefully the rider puts her foot in the stirrup and, with the holder steadying the stirrup so that the rider's foot does not poke the horse as she moves, swings gently onto his back. We do this several times and, providing the horse is happy, then remove the bucket and re-mount from the ground. Our agile rider is needed again, as it is very important to move as smoothly as possible and stay close to the horse. Any sudden movements or pull on his side could frighten him, and a rider with one foot in the stirrup is in a potentially dangerous situation until she is aboard. If time is taken to build up the horse's trust in the rider *before* trying to mount from the ground with the stirrup, however, then there is generally no problem.

Riding in Company

Right from the first day we must keep in mind that the horse is going to have to perform a job that requires courage, and he must develop the correct attitude. We want him ultimately to be bold and sensible, and he must not learn to hide and let others take on the problems now. So his schoolmaster must be there to help – but not always to lead him.

Each day we still do a little lungeing at first, just to make sure he is not going to panic and buck when he first moves on with the rider. Then we ride him in the school alone for the first few days. I like to keep the horse on a long rein, and only do twenty metre circles and simple change of reins, in all three paces. The day we introduce company we first work the horse by himself, and then bring our schoolmaster/older horse in to join in.

When he first comes in we let the yougster just follow behind. This can be quite exciting for him, and a schoolmaster who will not kick the young horse if he runs into his backside is essential. When they are both settled and trotting quietly around the school the older horse circles, and I move up on the ground as before and we encourage the baby to go large alone. The schoolmaster's rider now wants to keep the distance between the two horses equivalent to about half the school apart so that both horses, although in company, are working alone. If the young one rushes or stops I help on the ground, and the schoolmaster still maintains the half school distance. When both are settled like this, then we start one or the other circling quietly, to come up behind the other and then turn away again. So literally from day one we are making sure our future cross-country horse is developing the correct attitude for working alone, boldly and bravely. A youngster should never develop the 'sheep-like' attitude of following the older horse – it can be terribly difficult to break later on, so why allow it to become a habit now? Taken firmly and quietly, with a good rider and an experienced person on the ground, I have never known any major problems and have always had our youngsters working happily and independently like this on the very first day in company.

When the youngster is quite happy to work away from the other horse we go outside, and just ride together to the end of our lane (about a quarter of a mile) and back. The youngster is encouraged to go ahead, but the schoolmaster is there ready to go on and lead him if he hesitates at first. Just a short ride for this first time, but still a big day – and from now on I will feel that he is truly rideable. At about this stage we will start to cut out lungeing before riding when we feel it is no longer necessary.

Every day we ride out for short periods outside. The aim is to encourage a positive reaction to new places: I do not like to force my young horse to go in front, but praise him when he does so and let him think it is fun. It is so important now to have both a good schoolmaster *and* a rider who is experienced with young horses on him. If I am on the older horse I watch the young one's reactions all the time, and even when he is in front I make sure I am only a half length behind, so that in the early stages if he hesitates at something alarming I just walk on past, he follows and, with his rider urging him on almost immediately, we are both past and he is back in front before he realises it. I never, ever like to engage in a battle that cannot be won, and at this early stage the commands will not be well enough established to meet him head on in a fight. For the same reason, in the first few days we go to easy places for our short rides.

Riding Out

After four or five days like this it is time for a proper hack out. We usually go into the school for five minutes to make sure the horse is as rideable as normal, then off we go. I like to go for quite a reasonable ride the first time, for about an hour, so that being ridden becomes established as a serious job and the youngster does not have the time (or excess energy) to think of causing trouble next time. A good pair of 'nannies' – both horse and rider – are needed again to do the same job as with our early short rides out. Through strange fields or farms I again like to encourage our baby to go past strange, horrid things first, and each time we see a spooky thing push this a little more – but in these early days we still try to keep to fairly horror-free rides. After a few days, when he is confident in taking the lead, we ride him out around a ride he knows alone. I do this as soon as possible so that he gets used to the idea of working alone at times and not always in company. With new rides or nasty places I would still always take him in company, but I do like to work our youngsters alone about fifty per cent of the time.

Around now we start to play at 'cross-country'. We have several places near us where there are little slopes and banks, or narrow spooky paths and stream or river crossings. The older horse goes first, and the young one follows the first time; then next time he goes by himself. Nothing too ambitious at this stage, just different places which are slightly tricky.

1

2

Riding out Time for the first ride outside, and the schoolmaster is already positioned in front to give a lead (1). To start with (2) just going along behind is an effort, but very quickly (3) Dodger is striding confidently on ahead, although later the schoolmaster is needed for a lead past the spooky tyres (4).

3

4

Paths in woods are ideal – it is rather like encouraging small children to take the initiative and explore new places, looking on to see what is around every corner. When the youngster is quite happy to lead the way, we are en route to the right eventing attitude.

For the next couple of months I like to establish completely that the horse is quite confident to hack out both alone and in company. We try to find new places to go to avoid his life becoming boring, and try not to do too much actual schooling as such – although virtually every day he is being 'schooled' to be a better riding horse. We work at all paces, though on the roads we mostly walk and just trot up the hills to reduce the jar. When we can find nice lanes with good going (few and far between in our area) we canter on and generally let the horse develop a forward going attitude. If it is possible to turn the youngster out in the field for a few hours each day it will do him the world of good, helping to occupy his mind and allowing him to buck and play if he wants to – and hopefully get it out of his system. Like most people, though, we do suffer from limited grazing and so cannot always do this. One day to have limitless horse paddocks for turning out would be bliss.

Tack and Clothing

Bits

The saddlery and equipment that I use on a young horse is fairly simple. My favourite bit to start with is a jointed rubber snaffle, which gives a little more 'steering power' than a straight bar rubber snaffle but is still mild enough for a soft baby mouth. I might, however, use a straight bar or mullen mouthed rubber bit if my youngster was not happy in a jointed bit. Bitting always has to be flexible, and what suits one horse will not necessarily work on another; they are all shaped differently and may be comfortable in many different designs of mouthpiece. Trial and error and observing how happy they are with their bit is the only answer.

The bit should be accepted – and fit properly – from the lungeing stage onwards. Having either cheekpieces of some sort or 'D' cheeks on a young horse's bit can help enormously in turning, and if he really sets himself one way or another is not so easy to pull the bit right through the mouth. That can happen, and trying to stay in control with the rein in the horse's mouth can be very tricky!

With nosebands, I prefer one with some sort of 'dropped' action. I am quite happy with any of these, either a grackle (crossed) noseband, a 'flash', or the conventional dropped noseband. This is put on fairly loosely, but it is useful to have it there just to discourage the horse from really opening his mouth. It also helps keep the bit in the centre of the mouth if he is very reluctant about turning. But again, as with bits, all horses are different, and it is not that unusual to find a horse who will resist and fight any noseband other than a cavesson. If he will go well in this then I am quite happy to work him in it – my Master Fiddler wears a loosely fastened cavesson for all his work, including jumping and cross-country. He can be very strong and when he does pull he opens his mouth, so when I first bought him and discovered this across country I tried a grackle. Although he then kept his mouth shut he also set his jaw totally, and was far stronger than before. A few more experiments with different nosebands and it was back to the loose cavesson, which was definitely the best for him, and still is.

Saddles

As for saddles, I always ride in a Pennwood lightweight. I love a lightweight jumping saddle, and although I have tried many sorts of saddles have always returned to these (except for dressage with the older horses). A heavy saddle must feel odd to a young horse, and also I like to feel as close as possible to my horse, which the lighter saddles do allow. We use thin cotton numnahs, with pads of foam running just under the seat of the saddle. This gives a good thick numnah on the horse's back, but very little beneath the saddle flaps between my legs and the horse. Thin numnahs are also easy to wash, and we can then keep a supply of clean ones available. A sore back would be a real disaster when working on a young horse – he would either be uncomfortable and resistant if kept working or would have to have a break, neither of which is good news – and a dirty, sweaty numnah will quickly cause this. For similar reasons we use material girths that feel soft and are easily cleaned.

Martingales

I do not generally use a martingale at this stage. It is important to know that the horse is carrying himself correctly without relying on a martingale, and a running martingale, however loose, does have a slight pulley effect which alters the normal contact. It can also make steering very difficult at times, and it is for this reason that I will never use one at first in cross-country competitions if it can be avoided. I would rather have a high head carriage at times and direct contact, than the feeling of the martingale allowing my horse to drift and wander.

A standing martingale can become a virtual 'prop' for the young horse to lean on, and I do not like the use of them for this reason. I have known young horses who have been ridden in standing martingales and learnt to hang on them, and invariably as I have lengthened the martingale their heads have gone higher to pick up the contact again – not easy to correct.

But, again, an exception. Merry Sovereign was a very naughty youngster, and used to throw his head up and down when excited on the way home until he managed to get his whole body doing virtual caprioles in time with his head. We would then arrive home in a series of enormous leaps, *very* fast. I put on a loose standing martingale which never came into contact at all – until the first head throw on the way to capriole. 'Snap' it went on his nose with amazing force – and Sovereign behaved. But I still used it *only* when riding out, so that neither of us become reliant on it, and kept it very loose so that it only came into use when he was very silly. I am not anti-martingale (or any bit) in later days if they work in competition, but in the early days it is best to keep it simple.

Boots

Front boots should always be used with a young horse. I have some marvellous ones made in Holland that have a hard polystyrene sleeve running down the back of the precious tendons, with a chrome-type leather covering which fastens with velcro, encasing and protecting the front of the cannon bone. These guard against brushing, and prevent injury from the horse striking into himself or hitting a pole when jumping. If his action causes him to brush behind then we can put on a boot behind, but I do not use back boots at home all the time. I always carry a whip: with a horse who sees it and is frightened then I will take a very short, dark-coloured one, but I never ride without. When it is needed to back up my commands it is a vital piece of equipment, and must be there.

For early competitions back leg boots can be added for the cross-country, plus over-reach boots for this and the showjumping. I use very short over-reach boots which we cut down to about half length ourselves. I am convinced that Master Fiddler fell well after landing at the Croft at Gatcombe in 1988 because he stepped on his own boot – so we have very short ones to help protect the coronet and yet not be long enough to step on. I use only these additional items of protection away from home because if we get into trouble competing I am going to have to ride forward out of it to the next fence – we cannot circle around as we might at home, and may well hit the fence in doing so, when my boots will save an injury.

Essential Extras

I like to use a breastplate and surcingle as well for cross-country – it is not pleasant to find the saddle disappearing as we go. And of course I will add my back protector to my clothes, as well as my faithful crash hat which I always wear. I do wear spurs across country in competition (but not generally for show jumping) as I like to have an extra surprise up my sleeve if my youngster does spook at his first ditches or water in public!

3 · 'BABY' WORK

Once the young horse is established as a safe and confident ride, we can start to tackle the schooling with more concentration. I usually school seriously not more than three times a week, but if there is a problem I may school two or three days in a row. I tend to work my youngsters for about 1-1¼ hours, and in their early stages this is the total amount of work they do. Later on in their career when we are approaching an event I will do my schooling time as *well* as my roadwork, as at that stage I want to build up my horse's fitness, whereas at this stage schooling for forty minutes will probably tire him far more than an hour's hacking.

At first we want the horse to settle on a loose rein, to begin with at walk and trot and then, when that is established, at canter as well. Here, we put motor tyres in the corners of the school, which are a big help in keeping youngsters out around the track. Try to pick up the rein only to adjust your steering at first, and if the horse rushes just circle, talking to him quietly until he settles, and then gradually extend the circle until you are going large again. I do like my horses to find their own balance and pace before establishing too much of a contact; it can only be the source of potential problems if they have not. The horse who is forever being steadied by the hand will always tend to lean and use the rider as a fifth leg, and he will find it very difficult to come off his forehand and develop true self-carriage. Similarly, the idle horse who is always being ridden forward with every stride will be difficult to train to be truly obedient to the leg. If a horse is lazy, use a schooling whip to follow up your leg aids – we want him going forward by himself in a settled fashion, while the rider has a fairly neutral effect on his way of going.

On the Bit

After this we have to begin thinking about the rider starting to actually ride the horse up onto a contact and have him on the bit. It the horse is carrying himself properly and has good basic conformation this should not be too difficult. We continue to ride in the school in the same rhythm, and gradually pick up a contact through the reins with the horse's mouth, at the same time quietly starting to push him forward with the legs onto the bridle. Nothing too ambitious, just going large and a few twenty metre circles as before. You can still use your voice to back up your legs and hands, particularly in the transitions from one pace to another. Let the horse take his time when changing pace; I like to think of how he takes his time on the lunge. When lungeing, we give the command with our voice, he thinks about it and with no actual physical interference from us learns to change pace evenly and in balance. I hate to see young horses hassled into doing a transition immediately they are asked – rather, we ask quietly with voice and body and let them take their time, while maintaining their self-carriage. There is a lot for them to think about and work out, but each time the change comes more easily and quickly. And we do need good flowing transitions, not only ultimately for good dressage marks, but also for quick, economical jumping.

The aim now is to establish the horse going in a long low outline, accepting the bit and working on a good contact, but still maintaining this outline so that he is stretching down onto the bit. I like to work at all paces, and think it is easier to do this early flat work in the confined area of the school. Youngsters find concentrating very difficult, and the school is usually easier for them to work in as there are fewer distractions. A wall or rails around the schooling area always seems to help – I have often noticed how much better a young horse will carry himself with the security of the wall beside him.

Schooling Outside

Once we are happy with the way the horse is going inside, we can take him outside and school there. Eventually he is going to have to do his dressage tests outside, and the sooner he realises he can work in the fields the better. We are lucky to have some nice level fields to school in; unlevel ground is very difficult for youngsters, and if we did not have our own flat areas I would be prepared to hack or even box to level ground at this stage.

For the first schooling session outside we can again take out an older horse as schoolmaster. Most youngsters seem to find circling in the middle of a field quite baffling to begin with, as up to now in their lives, whether grazing loose or being ridden they have only gone across fields for a purpose, and being asked to go around and around for no apparent reason can cause confusion – with a strong character this can result in a tantrum as he refuses to co-operate. As total control is still not completely established at this stage, we can use our schoolmaster once more to make things easier. I have found that the best method is to ride to the field together, and then just let the older horse stand in the centre while the youngster works around him. The mere presence of a steadying influence in the middle seems to have a settling effect, and even the more tricky characters are quite happy to work like this without the confines of a school to help them. I may well not let the older horse join in and school with the youngster on the first day, but will simply establish his work again and then next time school them together. Once we can school the youngster either alone or in company, both in the school and outside, we can start his jumping schooling – the really fun part.

Trotting poles (1) To start with, Dodger is rather 'hollow' and tense; he is almost rushing and is not yet at all confident. After working quietly over the poles for several circuits, however, he has settled and is now (2) active and round, and is quietly looking down and stretching towards the final pole.

First Jumping Lessons

Working Over Poles

My first lesson towards jumping is to get the horse to work over poles on the ground. I like to go back into the school and start first of all with just one pole on the long side of the arena. We just walk over it at first, which is often interesting, since as far as the horse is concerned a pole has suddenly materialised on the track! Some laid-back individuals almost seem not to notice, but some are most suspicious of this pole which can obviously walk and must have a life of its own! Firmly and quietly, I will insist he walks on and steps over it, and repeat this until he is stepping over it in his normal walk. I very rarely use a schoolmaster to give a young horse a lead at this stage, as his ultimate job will be to jump alone and I prefer to go very slowly with him by himself now. Once he is walking nicely over one pole, we put out another at a distance of about 4ft 6in from the first pole and get him to walk over both. The distance is not quite right for walking, but it is best to leave the poles in the same position so they have not 'walked' when we go into trot. As we start to trot it is important to keep the horse quiet, as we do not want him to think of leaping or jumping over the poles, but just to trot gently over them in an even rhythm.

What we are looking for in our early pole work is to establish the basic principle of jumping. The horse's eventual jump is the conclusion of his approach, and the approach to the next fence will start as he is in the air over the jump before, so this is one of the most important stages in our horse's career. Doing pole and ground work will be an essential part of his training throughout his competitive life, and he must learn to do it correctly now. The right attitude to jumping must also be taught – it is great fun, but should cause no more excitement or rushing than any other work. The really natural jumper will love the sensation of jumping, and this enthusiasm must be kept going, but under control! We want our horse to approach his poles as he will his fences: straight and in an even rhythm. Any tendency to wander from a straight line must be corrected on the approach, over the pole and on 'landing', and any attempt to quicken and rush or slow down and hesitate should also be quietly and firmly stopped.

Once we have our young horse trotting nicely over two poles, we can add a third pole at the same distance and then, when that is easy, put down a fourth pole 9ft away from the third. He then has to put in a whole trot stride within that distance, all four of his feet, and will be positioned exactly right to take off and jump when the fourth pole is made into a small fence. There is no hurry at this stage, and if the horse feels good over the four poles we can stop at that point, and then next time actually jump. By doing this we have started to confirm that poles are part of normal schooling and not something exciting.

The First Jump

Next time we are going to jump we confirm our last trotting pole lesson, and then add another pole to the fourth to make them into a tiny cross pole. Very often a scopey horse will just elevate his stride a little more and merely trot over this, which is something of an anti-climax. We then build it into a small vertical fence with a pole slightly in front of it on the ground (about six inches away, no more). As the rider, my job is to keep the horse straight, and be ready to press him forward if he loses his even rhythm. I have learnt to sit very still on landing when the horse does jump. Quite often the feeling of the rider, however careful we are, leaving the saddle as he jumps and coming back onto his back can cause panic in a nervous horse, so I use a lot of voice and try to move as little as possible – he has enough to think about with negotiating the jump without being wary of the object on his back. Quietly I circle and get him back to his good trot rhythm and round we come again. Two or three nice jumps over our little upright jump are plenty the first day, and I like to dismount and make a fuss of him and put him back to bed feeling like a star.

We stay with our trotting pole exercise for the next few lessons and then next time, after jumping the vertical jump well, we put in another pole to make a small spread fence. This should be slightly higher than the front pole so that he can see it easily, and should have very little width so that it is not alarming. We can use the same colour pole so that he does not

1 2

The first fence Now (1) we can add another pole, and Dodger looks ahead to his little jump and (2) hops over rather carefully, but nicely. With a proper jump (3) he looks good again, and then (4) finishes (rather seriously – real baby concentration) with a small spread.

3

4

spook and frighten himself. Again, if this is jumped nicely that is enough for that day. When this jump has built up into a parallel 2ft high and is being jumped nicely and confidently, then we move onto another lesson. As with the flat work, I only jump a few times a week, and still go out for our hacks in different places all the time.

The First Solid Fence

I like to tackle a solid jump next, before jumping two fences in a row – our first grid.

The first solid fence should be as easy as possible. We have a tried and trusted method for this that has worked well with all our young ones. We use a row of three forty-gallon drums, and initially remove the centre drum so that we have a gap in the middle. We walk – or attempt to! – through this gap to start with. It is important to remember that so far in the horse's life solid objects have been avoided and by-passed, so that to have to actually approach within a few inches of one can be quite alarming. We walk through this gap several times until the horse is quite confident, and then trot between the drums. When he is trotting through nicely, we then put a small five-gallon drum into the middle. Now I, as the rider, really have to concentrate! I try to think of both reins almost as tram lines to keep my horse straight, and I keep my hands low and apart, almost having both reins as 'open' reins. I should be slightly behind his movement, ready to ride him forward if he hesitates and keep him straight if he tries to run out. I am quite unashamed to admit that I find 'stoppers', who will refuse if in doubt, quite frightening to ride into fences – and from day one my future star is not going to be allowed to *consider* a hesitation or refusal. If the worst happens and he does stop, he must *not* be allowed to run away, but must be punished 'at the scene of the crime'. The rider's job is to keep him in front of the fence, and I like to hit him hard with the whip behind my leg *once*. Then re-approach, and be doubly determined we are going. A young horse should virtually never stop, and when they do I worry about why, and what I did wrong – but still tell them they were very naughty! Throughout my good horses' whole career (from baby to star) you could count their refusals on one hand – and that is the way it must be.

So, when we are hopping happily over the little drum, the same day we change it to the third original drum. With a couple of helpers in the school this can be done with the minimum of fuss, and hopefully without the horse noticing. I ride at the fence again, 200 per cent behind him but without hurrying, and should be rewarded with a confident jump over his first really solid obstacle. From now on he will have to tackle solid jumps without the baby introduction, but after several fights years ago with non-understanding youngsters kneeling on their first fence like this in panic, I like to use this method initially. Then there can be no excuse next time.

For the next lesson I like to jump my drum, jump again and then jump another, different drum fence. Then again probably one more jump with another colour of drum, and then (very aware of no stops again) some other new fence – possibly our planks or a board filler under a rail, but at a very tiny height. I confirm that new and different small jumps are no problem for a few lessons, and then we start to tackle two fences in a row – our first piece of gridwork.

First Combinations

To start with, we place two poles on the ground at a distance of 9ft apart. To the side of the second pole we stand a pair of jump wings or uprights, ready to turn the second pole into a small placing fence. Then, at a distance of 20ft away from the second pole, we have another pair of uprights in position to make our second fence in turn. We always measure the distance *inside* the grid – that is, from the second pole on the ground (which will become the first jump) to the front pair of uprights (which will become the front rail of the second jump) of the final fence. We put several poles and jump cups nearby, and then everything is set up for us to begin.

As with our earlier lessons, first of all we settle the horse at trot in an even rhythm on a straight line over the two poles. Now that we are thinking of two fences, without hopefully running out at the second, we want to ensure that our horse is absolutely confirmed in maintaining his straight line on through the sets of uprights and away. Once he is trotting nicely over the poles, we add another rail and make a small cross pole jump from the uprights. This is built up to a small upright jump, between 18in and 2ft high, and when the horse has hopped over this nicely we are ready for a second jump. We build a similar size fence on the front pair of uprights we positioned earlier, with a ground rail slightly in front of it – again, about 6in away – to make it easy for our horse. Now, we can make another 'first time of' lesson even easier. We bring the horse into the second fence, only we do this by turning in slowly on a little angle and just asking him to pop over quietly. As by now he has jumped several different new single fences in earlier lessons this should be no problem, and we let him jump the fence two or three times like this until he is quite confident with it. I always do this when tackling a combination of jumps for the first time, in order to avoid the possibility of frightening my youngster. It is only too easy for young horses to be so busy looking at this strange second fence which has suddenly materialised from nowhere that they literally fall

Grid An early grid lesson for Sweep the Board. Here (1) he is looking keenly up at the first fence and makes a nice jump over it (2). As he lands (3) the uprights for the second fence are in position, and he is looking ahead and at them correctly. When we add a second jump, he is 'backing off' slightly in his one non-jumping stride (4) but, pushed on by the rider, makes a good jump (5).

1

2

3

4

5

3

Grid with spread By the time we have added a spread, Sweep the Board is going forward much better in between the two obstacles (1), and (2 & 3) puts in a lovely, scopey, correct jump. An excellent lesson.

through the first fence, having never even glanced at it – and for that to happen at the first attempt is not going to help their confidence!

Once both jumps have been popped over, we then have to put them together. To start with we make the first fence back into a small crosspole, so that it really needs very little jumping. It is absolutely vital that the horse does not learn now that he can 'duck out' and avoid the second jump, and this is what we are mostly concentrating on – that we stay straight and get over the second fence somehow. How many strides we have between the jumps and even how he jumps is not so important, but he must learn *now* to go forward and tackle what is in front. It is in these earliest jumping lessons that the horse learns that he is expected to go between the wings of the fence and face the problems ahead: bravely, at the first attempt and without hesitation. *How* he does this is up to him, but any horse with the ability to jump is going to learn to negotiate what is in front of him in the most efficient way – leap over it! 'Having a look' and then going next time is *not* clever. Later on, at all levels of competition, he will not be able to have a look and go – if he does, he will either frighten himself one day when he sees a nasty hole in the ground under a fence, or

2 1

find he has looked so much that there is no impulsion left and he jumps right into the hole. Looking and hesitating is a recipe for potential disaster. The first few jumping lessons are when, hopefully, we will develop our horse's ultimate attitude of 'Yes, madam, we are on and jumping' whenever we approach strange obstacles.

GRIDS

Once we have managed to negotiate both fences together, next time we can concentrate more on ensuring we have a nice single stride of non-jumping canter between the jumps. The distance is perfect for this when approached at trot, and when the horse is confident with the fences this comes very easily, usually on the first few attempts. If he is happy then we put the first jump back up to the original size, and we are then actually jumping a real grid exercise. Depending on the horse, we may finish this lesson with both jumps as small uprights or may add a back pole to the second and finish with a small parallel or oxer out of the combination. If we had not finished with an oxer the first time, this would be the lesson we would build up to the next time.

One other basic grid exercise we can use when our horse is totally confident over two fences is an upright one stride after a parallel. We have our parallel fence following three trotting poles, and with these two exercises alternated with different single fences it is enough to teach and confirm the young horse's jumping style. We build him up over the trotting poles to a small upright fence, then add a back rail to this and have a small parallel. The second jump we put 18ft away from our trotting pole parallel. This distance is a little shorter than in my earlier basic grid, as I have found that horses do not jump out as far over the spread as they do over the small placing fence. Keep the first jump small with little spread to start with, as again we do not want the youngster to be so busy looking at the second jump that he jumps into the first, and have the new fence just a little higher than the first so that he can see it clearly. Over several sessions we can then build these two grid combinations up to a slightly bigger jump.

Although I may use other combinations to keep my horses athletic and clever, these two are the exercises I find I use most and can recommend as the most consistently successful.

The First Double

The next lesson is to jump a proper double, with no gradual build up. Start with two upright fences, as they are easier to get away with jumping badly if the horse does try to stop or run out. I do not have as long a distance between the fences as we will have in competition, as I like my horses to establish their one non-jumping stride easily – about 22ft 6in works best. Keep both jumps small, about 2ft high at the most, and trot in slowly, making sure you are slightly behind the movement ready to correct any hesitation or drifting to one side. As with the first grid, we are not so concerned about *how* the horse jumps – so long as he does both fences at the first attempt! I like to jump this little double from both directions, and when my youngster is confident this is another lesson learnt. Next time we lengthen the distance a little, as ultimately we want him to be happy with 24ft as one stride.

Jumping a Course

Stringing all these different lessons together into an actual course of fences comes next. I do like to jump a variety of 'spooky' fences, such as small walls and solid fillers, and if I cannot find enough funny-looking jumps anything safe will serve the purpose. It is amazing if you look around how cardboard boxes, rubber containers and all sorts of other things can make interesting fences – the everyday economy version of the Seoul Olympic show jumps, and only 2ft high! I like to build a course of baby fences with a double and as many different-looking fences as possible, and then jump around the course without repeating individually any fences which do not go perfectly – after all, when we go out and compete we will not be able to circle and repeat a bad jump. Unless every fence was foot perfect (very rare), I then immediately go around my course again while my horse still remembers the jumps and hopefully will find them easier. This I will aim to do at my first few shows with clear round showjumping, and these early little home courses are really dress rehearsals for later days.

4 · EARLY CROSS-

COUNTRY TRAINING

A young horse's earliest cross-country training is really only an extension of riding out across strange country. The same basic principles of going quietly forward when there are problems ahead has to be established now, with small obstacles to cope with on the way.

Water

How to cross water is one of the most important lessons for the young horse to learn. We are very lucky to have a river running through our land, and there are several places where we can go in and out. The young horse should always have a schoolmaster to follow into water the first time – it is quite natural and normal for him to be afraid of going into water initially, for how can he possibly know that there is a bottom to it and that it is safe? The only way a horse can learn that water is safe is to build up trust in his rider, and this can only happen by taking him into shallow places with a good bottom and teaching him that nothing awful will happen.

The surface beneath the water must be inspected carefully before being ridden into. A boggy, soft bottom will feel sinky and unsafe and would be enough to frighten any horse – the last thing that should happen to a youngster with his first venture into water. The bank or edge of the water should also be firm, as if it feels as though it is about to give way it is bound to discourage him from going anywhere near the water, and if he does go in it will teach him to be very cautious at the edge. This, when we want to encourage him one day to jump into a proper water jump, is not an awfully good idea.

The surfaces both in and edging the water must be good in order to encourage the horse to feel that he can accelerate into it, rather like children whizzing down a slide and enjoying the splash. Going in with company also helps teach the youngster that he can play in water and have fun; we are very lucky here as we can go into the river often when we ride out, and all our horses love splashing and playing about. In fact when we get to the field where we go most often into the river, if we drop the reins on the older horses they will trot off by themselves straight into the water – and Dazzle positively charges in.

First Lessons

For our first water lesson we go off into the field with one or two guaranteed water-lovers as schoolmasters. Our young horse wants to be encouraged to stay right up behind his friend and just follow on in. We only walk at first, and it is very important for the rider to be slightly behind the horse, ready to keep him facing the river and prevent him from turning around and running away if he tries to. If he does stop and refuse to go forward, then he must be kept facing the water and urged forward with the rider's legs and voice, and with little taps of the whip behind the leg. I do not mind bringing the schoolmaster out past him and then back in again, if necessary several times, so he sees that it is both possible and safe. Sometimes when a young horse stops on the edge of water he seems to become almost transfixed on the brink, staring at the edge almost as if he feels he has to dive into this water-filled, bottomless pit. Watching the others walk in and out, and maybe one horse wandering around already in there, seems to help make him realise that it really will be alright to go in. 'Come on in, the water's lovely' is the message we are trying to convey to the horse.

When he does decide to go, the rider must sit tight. It is not unusual at all for a youngster to leap in – almost mentally holding his nose like a diver – and I have had horses who have jumped again as they felt the water (I can remember one who did a real rodeo act as soon as the cold water hit his tummy). These antics do disappear quite quickly though, as the horse begins to realise that it is only water and does not really hurt, but I always like to be ready for fireworks when I ride into water for the first time with each young horse just in case.

Once the horse is in the river then he must be encouraged to walk about. Right from day one we want him to learn to find his balance with the pull of the water; eventually we will trot and canter and even jump in there, and he must start to develop the balance to do this. Moving about will also help him to think of water as something normal. Often the bubbles and spray will be frightening at first; I like to let my horses sniff and blow bubbles, and if they paw and splash as well that is great – it should be fun in there. Moving forward bravely into, across and out of expanses of water is what we are after, but that will only happen when our horse is totally confident and happy.

When he is standing without concern in the river, them we will all go out and come back in again, with the youngster following the others. We will do this as many times as necessary until there is no hesitation, and then take him out alone and back in again by himself, but towards his friends who are still in the water. When this is going well then we will all go out, and this time he has to go in alone without a lead. This final part of the first lesson is vital, so that the horse finishes by being totally brave all by himself (as he will have to be in competition), not following the others like a sheep.

1

Water I (1) Even following his schoolmaster, Dodger looks very hesitant, and actually halts to watch her walk on into the river to join the other horse. With quiet persuasion he decides (2) to be brave and follow, very suspiciously and

2 3

stiffly, but he still goes. Now (3) by himself he is finally very confident, his ears are pricked as he looks ahead and his body is far more relaxed. And then (4) he can tell the others just how clever he was.

4

For the next water lesson we return to the river and go in and play around as we did before. We must concentrate on making sure the young horse is really going forward as he gets to the edge of the water, and then we will think about actually jumping. The first water jump we use here is a small pole, about 2ft high, which is approximately 18ft from the river. It is right beside where we have been into the river before, and so does not involve jumping into the unknown. Any fence like this with a problem immediately on landing, in this case the river, is a 'coffin'-type fence – the classic coffin is a rail followed by a ditch and then another rail, but any jump with something to look at and assess beyond it can be ridden in a similar way. The horse must be given time to see what he has to do, so a steady approach is needed, but the rider must ride very strongly as these jumps are classic 'stoppers' – the horse thinks he has to jump right into the second problem, and does not realise he has room to land and go again. Once more, it is very important to keep slightly behind the movement and be ready to keep the horse straight, just keeping the leg on firmly so that he feels he can go when he sees there is room to land. Often a young horse will almost fall through or over the rail, so a secure lower leg from the rider is essential in order to keep himself in the saddle and in a correct position on landing. As he lands, the young horse will often try to veer sideways and avoid the river – even when he has been in before, another place is often quite alarming – and he must be kept straight and ridden on in. This fence can be jumped several times, and then we are ready actually to tackle a fence which puts us straight into the water.

TAKING THE PLUNGE

A straight forward small log or solid jump into water is the best first jump, and again needs to be approached slowly and firmly. The fence should be small enough for the horse to be kept in front of it if he does stop, and just pushed and chivvied until he decides to jump in. The rider's lower leg must be good and secure again if he does jump big, so that there is no chance of shooting over his head if he trips or stumbles, and the horse must be encouraged to move forward and away as he lands. A horse who stops dead on landing into water is very difficult to sit on; and in future we shall often want him to be ready to move across a water fence and jump out again at the other side.

Once the horse is quite happy jumping into water, we can think about teaching him to jump a rail actually *in* water – often not so easy to arrange, as quite a large expanse of water is needed. I like to put up a pole – a heavy, fat rail such as a telegraph pole is ideal – and have it clearly visible above the water. (We often take two oil drums and a big rail into our meadow when we have floods – brilliant practice, as the water is only shallow and the field makes a great surface.) The young horse should initially be allowed to just walk about, and then be encouraged to trot on and find his balance. Once he feels happy, he can then be ridden into the rail.

When jumping in water it is important to concentrate on keeping a good rhythm in a powerful trot. Often when approaching the jump the horse will look up at it and, with the pull of the water, lose his impulsion, realise he is not going forward enough and misjudge his takeoff, either throwing himself at the fence or running in too close and stopping. Strong riding is needed to keep him active and up together, and the temptation to interfere too much and tell him when to take off must be resisted. In water horses often take off in slightly unexpected places; our job as rider is to give them all our help if they do, and the best way we can do this is by keeping their activity going and ensuring that our weight is in a balanced position. If the horse does find jumping in water awkward we let him play around and jump the jump several times, and gradually learn how to cope. He will work it out.

The Jump Out

The last problem with water is jumping out. Almost every horse seems to find hopping up a bank out of water difficult at first, and even at the top level the most experienced horses often 'miss' at the smallest banks out of water. Many times at Badminton there have been falls when horses have literally tripped up the bank from the lake, and in the World Championships at Gawler there were several falls at a very small bank out of the water. Again, as with jumping into water, all the rider can really do is concentrate on keeping the horse as balanced and active as possible, and try to encourage him to look at the bank, think about it, get close and just pop up.

The worst problems come when the horse either launches himself far too early, or goes to do so and then changes his mind. If he does 'miss' and jumps badly, the rider must try to keep in balance and allow him freedom to recover: often he will almost 'belly flop' onto the bank and will need to regain his feet. Having made a mess of jumping out, we must hop back in again and let the horse just wander about in the water and relax, and then try again. After a few attempts it will generally dawn on him how to cope and make a neat jump out.

At home we will practise jumping into, out of and in water, and occasionally play around with combinations either going into or out of water. These do not usually present any great problem, and often make jumping into water easier as the horse will meet the actual fence into the water perfectly. It is often surprising that in competition it is not usually the combination but the difficult *single* fence into water that causes refusals.

1

Water II Having been into the river several times, Sweep the Board makes a lovely competent jump over the little drop (1). He is checking himself on landing as he watches his approach towards the river (2) but, ridden on straight, is going into the water very keenly (3). As he splashes in (4) he is putting his head up to

3

2

avoid the spray (rather like we hold our noses when jumping into a swimming pool) but once in (5) he obviously thinks it is fun and that he has been extremely clever.

4 5

1 2

Water III Here Halloween Time is showing how much our older horses love the river: it is a great treat to be allowed to go in and play, and marvellous practice for water obstacles in cross-country. It is interesting to see here how the more experienced horse readjusts his body weight, without interference from the rider, in order to maintain his balance correctly both up and down the slope and in the water.

5

3

4

When building combination fences with water for schooling it is important to remember that the horse will tend to be almost 'backing off' and shortening his stride as he approaches and is in the water, and the distance will need to be more like a trotting grid distance than that between cantering fences in order to allow for this.

Drop Fences

Drops are another new question to face. Down by our river we have a marvellous little 'cul-de-sac' at the edge of the field, which is where the river bank used to be years ago. At some stage in the river's life it changed its course and meandered away from the old path, leaving an expanse of sand with a sheer bank up into the field. The bank varies in height and with a selection of fences built along it we have a fantastic learning ground for drops, starting with baby slopes and going up to proper BHS event-sized drops – all with a lovely soft landing.

A good surface to jump onto is so important when teaching young horses. Landing on stony or very hard ground will inevitably be discouraging, however brave the horse – it is going to hurt, and if they are sensible they will quickly learn to say 'no thank you'. We want to encourage our horse to jump well out when he is jumping from one level to another: the further out he goes the smaller the angle at which he will hit the ground, and that will lessen the jar of jumping down. If he drops straight down like a stone it will feel a lot more jarring. Obviously, if the ground on landing slopes away from the fences we do not want to encourage him to jump too far out – this would definitely *increase* the drop – but we can ride him differently according to each fence and teach him to jump right out confidently when we tell him to do so. And for this we need a good landing.

All we ask the horse to do the first time we go down the bank is to walk down the slope beside the actual drop jumps. This slope is quite steep but very short, and by going down here without actually having to jump we have removed any possible fear of going along the lower level, so when we then ask the horse to take on the smallest drop jump he has no excuse for saying no.

Once the horse is quite happy to go down and up the slope then it is time to ask him to jump. A slow, balanced approach is needed, and again an almost backward-feeling seat in order to be right behind him if he does try to stop and evade the problem. The first proper drop fence should be small enough so that if he is reluctant he can be kept in front of the jump and pushed forward until he does jump from a standstill. I hate to turn around and come again at any fence, and if I can possibly avoid doing so I will. The horse must learn that he has to tackle every problem *first* try, and even if it takes a while to make him go over or into whatever we are asking, by not turning away he has in his mind gone at the first attempt – even if it would have merited a refusal in competition. From the small drop we will move to the one beside it which is slightly bigger, and by the time we have finished our first lesson he is doing a proper drop jump.

Now we want to find as many different drop-type fences as possible – not big ones, but different ones. In the fields and woods around here we have several places where animals have for years made paths up and down a variety of slopes, some going from field to field with quite a distinct drop and change of height. We go up and down these quite often, almost playing, so that the young horses learn to balance themselves while clambering up and sliding down. Most people can find a wood somewhere near them and teach their horses to be clever with funny places, and it will be so much easier then to cope with these sorts of places when they are set in competition. Once our young horse is confident (and is trusting his rider when he is asked to disappear over a nasty-looking place where he cannot see the landing), we can then introduce the coffin-type question of a fence just before the drop, and he can learn – as with the water – that it is safe to jump a fence carefully yet bravely with the slope beyond.

Banks

A bank jump is a natural progression on from learning about drops. We have a super bank, built fairly recently, which is a 21ft square platform. It is constructed out into the field as an extension to the existing hedge, which had a solid bank base, and on the side which is in line with the hedge has a ditch to jump in front of the bank or behind, depending on which direction we are going. It can be jumped from any direction, and with the natural slope of the field has varying heights to tackle. We start by trotting into it downhill, where it is about 2ft high. Rather like jumping up out of water, sometimes a young horse will misjudge and take off too far away – a horse I had a few years ago, Chevalier Noir, who went on to be a top class Advanced horse, tended to do this when he first started – and when a horse has launched himself at the bank in this way he may then belly flop onto the top. All that can be done by the rider to help prevent this is to try yet again to keep the horse in a good, balanced trot, and resist the temptation to chase him at the fence. Given time, the youngster will learn to get close and just hop up onto the bank, and then we must be ready to rebalance and help him on the top, and be behind him to ensure that he keeps straight and jumps down off again boldly.

1

2

4

3

First drop fence Here our real baby walks down the slope that he has been down several times before quite happily and then we ask him to jump the little drop and – trouble (1). Holly, riding, has the right rein and is ready for him, and quickly has him back in front of the fence (2) and is well behind him. His ears are back and he quite obviously is not too keen, but creeps forward slowly. Eventually he decides to go (3), and although the rider's weight and body are behind the movement she is giving him enough freedom of rein to make a good jump. When they approach again (4) his ears are pricked forward and he looks much happier, and at the following attempt he jumps big and confidently (5).

5

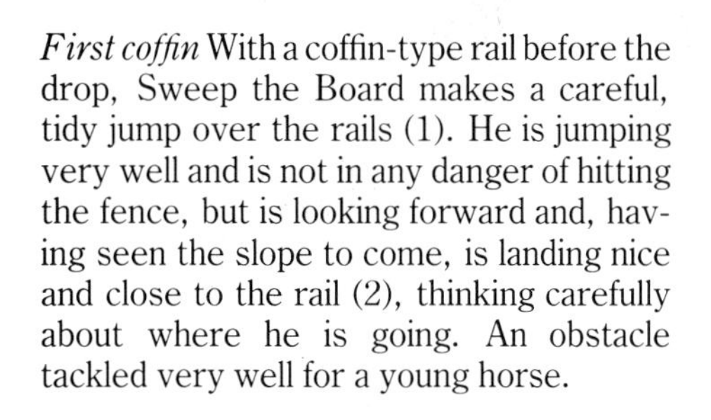

2

First coffin With a coffin-type rail before the drop, Sweep the Board makes a careful, tidy jump over the rails (1). He is jumping very well and is not in any danger of hitting the fence, but is looking forward and, having seen the slope to come, is landing nice and close to the rail (2), thinking carefully about where he is going. An obstacle tackled very well for a young horse.

1

1 2 3

Banks A good jump (1) onto the bank at the first attempt, but then the horse sees the drop at the far end (2) and steadies himself. The rider is allowing him to look at the problem (3) but is still well behind him, with the lower leg pushing him on. He jumps off in a most exaggerated way (4), going too high and not far enough

8

4 5

out, and the rider looks caught and rather cautious, but by (5) has given him more freedom. Next time, from the other direction (6), he is going forward much better, and with the rider pushing him on strongly (7) he strides out and jumps off very well (8).

7 6

1 2

A more difficult bank Later on we take on the more difficult way, and (1) the horse leaps boldly over the ditch onto the bank, across the top and makes a good, well-calculated jump off (2 & 3). He has learnt banks well.

Once he is trotting happily and jumping confidently then we can canter, but we must still remember to try to take off close to the bank so that the horse has his hocks underneath him and can push himself up onto the top. If photographs of horses jumping banks are studied, it is noticeable that they have to jump higher than normal to be able to unfold their legs and land on the jump. Not only does this require a lot of physical power but the horse also needs brain power in order to think and work out that there is a different level to land on, and he must be given time to look and see what he has to do. Usually when trouble happens at banks at any level it is when they have been approached too fast, and the horse has not been able to assess the problem in time.

At all levels of competition we have Normandy Banks – so called after this type of fence had appeared in a three-day event in France – which are normal banks constructed like our schooling fence, but with a rail to jump up and out over on the top. Usually it is either a question of bouncing off

3

the bank immediately on landing on the top, or putting in a small stride on the top. We can add a rail to our bank when we are tackling it back into the field to teach our horse to jump these types of bank, but I have never had a problem with a horse meeting his first Normandy Bank providing he is already confident about the whole concept of banking. Usually, in fact, if you watch a bold horse jump off a bank he would clear a small rail on the edge anyway.

The other type of bank that can be met in competition is a very narrow-topped, grass-covered bank, which does not really allow the horse to land properly on top but cannot easily be jumped right over. We do not have a baby version of one of these, but if a horse is already confident with banks and big solid fences, and is ridden into one of these banks in canter or trot with the rider keeping him steady and full of impulsion, he will decide how to jump it for himself. We cannot dictate where he will put his feet, and if he has done a lot of homework and played with different ground and tricky places he will make his own decision on how to jump these funny, rather ill-defined obstacles. Generally speaking, horses seem to jump them rather like dogs jump gates; they just push off behind in a sort of half banking system. But again an approach that is not too fast will help, as it will allow the horse to work out what he has to do.

Ditches

Ditches and water are the two most usual cross-country fences to which horses take an initial dislike. For schooling purposes we need a ditch which is neither too deep nor too wide, and has a clearly defined edge so that my horse will not slip into it and frighten himself. When riding at a ditch it is essential for the rider to keep looking up across it to the other side – my sister always used to say 'If you look down into the bottom of a ditch you will end up there'. At whatever level, once a horse (or for that matter a rider) has gazed down into the murky depths and had a thoroughly good look at what a nasty hole in the ground it is, it will be far more difficult to persuade him to jump over the yawning chasm. The rider must keep her eyes up, looking to the landing and where they are going afterwards, and encourage the horse to do exactly the same. The ditch should be small enough to jump from a standstill if our horse does stop, as yet again it is absolutely essential *not* to allow him to 'chicken out' and turn away for a second attempt. He is going to be a horse who always goes first time throughout his career – a really proper event horse.

Since ditches are initially quite alarming to most horses, for our very first lesson I allow the youngster to follow an experienced schoolmaster. If the young horse does get stuck in front of the ditch then the older one can come back and hop over again, several times if necessary, in order to give a lead and show that it really is possible and safe to jump. The ditch should be one that it is possible to pop over from both directions, and when the youngster has plucked up the courage to jump once he should be taken back and forwards over the same place until he is totally confident and unafraid. For the second ditch he tackles he must be alone: he now knows it is quite possible to jump across a hole in the ground, and he must get on and be brave and go by himself. From now on it is important to try to find as many small, safe ditches to jump over as possible, and the rider must try to go on rides where he can find little places to hop over so that our horse learns not to develop any ditch phobia.

Once a young horse is happy with small, straightforward ditches, we can then start to ask him to jump fences with ditches underneath, in front or behind. A trakener-type fence with a rail above the ditch, or an open ditch with a fence behind it, are actually far easier to ride than just plain, straightforward ditches. Having a jump to look at and ride to makes it far easier for horse and rider to resist the temptation to look down into the hole, and at any grade – even eventually at Advanced level – the maximum size of a ditch in front of or beneath the fence is easily within the horse's natural, normal jump. The rider must ignore the ditch completely and ride the fence boldly, and the horse will learn just to jump quite normally and disregard the ditch himself as well. Even if the rider feels the horse is going to get too close, the ditch must still be ignored; even the young horse will have the sense not to put his feet into it and will shorten his stride accordingly. With a fence in front of the ditch there will be a tendency for the horse not to take off too far away – and therefore not just over but also *into* the ditch, as the inexperienced rider is always convinced – but rather to be so busy looking at what is behind the jump that he consequently gets too close and hits the rail hard. It is really up to the rider not to 'throw' the horse at the fence, but to approach at a good, balanced, and quite steady pace and to keep him looking up at the fence, and then he will be able to work it all out and take off correctly as he assesses the problem.

Coffins

A real coffin is the last ditch problem we tackle. We have a rail that we can remove or add on one side of a small ditch, and to learn about coffins for the first time we remove the rail and jump the ditch alone to start with. When our horse has jumped this several times from both directions we will add the pole, and approach it with the ditch in front of the rail the first time.

The rider must now ride this somewhat like a Normandy Bank. I like to describe it as rather like when we were small and doing gym at school using a springboard: although we tried to get it right at the board it was all part of jumping over the horse, and when riding these sort of combination fences (this time on another sort of horse) we must convey this same feeling of continuation to our mount – we are jumping the ditch to jump the rail, not landing, then thinking again and falling over it. Both horse and rider must keep their eyes on the second jump as soon as they have started to jump the first and it will then feel easy. I like to jump this 'half coffin' several times from this direction, and then tackle it the difficult way with the rail before the ditch.

This is now the first real coffin for our youngster, and coffins at any level are always one of the most influential fences on the course, so we want to make it a good lesson. There is no reason why it shouldn't be, for we have taken the time and trouble to remove the fear of the unknown by jumping it the easy way first, and the horse can then concentrate on what he has to do now. Again we need a slow, balanced, straight and yet very strong approach, with the horse well between the rider's leg and hand.

First ditch Quite hesitant the first time (1), and although the rider has given him a lot of rein as he takes off (in a rather 'paddling' way) in mid-air (2) as he flattens his back and reaches out, the rein has contact again.

3 2

Half coffin Later, approaching from the opposite direction with a rail after the ditch (1) the horse is looking and going forward well, sorts his feet out quickly in the middle (2) and jumps out in good style (3). Half coffin and tiny Normandy bank learnt.

1 2

1

First coffin (1, 2 & 3) Coming back as a real coffin with the ditch after the rail, the young horse has really learnt his lesson well – and without the fright of being unsure of where he was going to land.

3

He must feel totally up together and active, and must not be chased so that he rushes. A few strides away these fences look no problem; the horse sees only the rail and will often want to accelerate at this easy-looking jump. Then, as he gets closer, he will see the ditch, and at first glance it will look exactly as if he cannot avoid jumping directly into it. If he has been allowed to start rushing before he arrives here it will be very easy for him to panic at this point and try to stop or run out, and if the rider has lost total control it will be very difficult to correct him. The rider must be ready to check him when he thinks it looks easy, and be right there ready to keep him going forward to the fence when it looks difficult; then at the last moment he will see that he does have room to land, and he can trust us and jump.

Sometimes a young horse will be untidy with his legs and hit the rail going into the coffin quite hard, but if he has been kept well balanced as he approaches it should not have too disastrous consequences. I like to praise the horse as soon as he has jumped and bring him straight back over it again with the ditch first, then turn and tackle the rail first for a second time. Once he is jumping both directions fluently, sensibly and with confidence then another lesson is over, and our next coffin can have a small jump both before and after the ditch and be tackled as one question at the first attempt. This should not present too much of a problem if the earlier lessons have been learnt, but the rider must concentrate on keeping the horse straight and up together all the way. What he does stride-wise is not very important although, as always, he must learn that he keeps going and jumps over all the problems ahead – first try, and with no run outs.

A Variety of Fences

Ditches, water, drops and banks have now all been tackled at baby heights, and although they are the major 'natural' cross-country fences to learn about, there are still a few different-looking jumps that can be practised at home. Logs for some extraordinary reason will often spook a young horse: a large dead-looking thing lying in the middle of a field can strike terror into his heart, and it is not a bad thing to practise at home and avoid the embarrassment of getting nowhere near the horse's first log in a competition. Any little logs that can be found at any stage in learning should be jumped, and even the spooky horse will soon realise that they are not tigers in disguise. Motor tyres often have a similar effect, and we have made a couple of small jumps out of them; they are only trotting height, and one of them is in fact one of our drop fences on the river bank, but they are still rather odd-looking and good practice.

A bullfinch is a good jump to have a small version of at home, and we built one several years ago. We used a single half sleeper as an upright on each end, and fastened rails on either side on the ground. Slit, half-round poles were then put either side of the uprights at a height of about 2ft 6in. We filled the gap between with thin cuttings from the hedges, from ground level to about 3ft high, until we had a thick untrimmed brush jump. The brush was then cut down level to about 2ft 9in – a good initial learning brush fence. We cut quite a few longer switches of lightweight brush-type sticks from the hedges, each about 6ft in length, and put a pile by the side of the small fence. We then jumped the brush, and then added just a few thin sticks to make a very sparse bullfinch to jump through. Starting like this with a very thin bullfinch seemed to present no real problems. At the time I had a horse who had always tried to jump right over this type of fence and consequently gave himself nothing but jarring landings from over-jumping. With this easy version he realised that he could brush through and although he still jumped big over thicker bullfinches he no longer tried to clear them.

With extra brush beside the fence it is quite easy to 'stiffen' it up by adding more to it, but I like to keep a schooling bullfinch fairly easy: a stiff, thick one is not nice to jump, and at home we want our lessons to be enjoyable. So we keep the nastier version for competition, and when our horse meets this with his adrenalin pumping as he jumps around a course he should jump it as confidently as the easier version at home.

Angles and Combinations

Natural fences such as these have always been problem fences at any level of cross-country competition, but so also are the combination and angle fences, both with and without natural features incorporated into them, and our young horse must start to learn about these as well. There is no necessity to be schooling outside to tackle these jumps, and in fact I think they are initially easier to learn in the school than outside.

My first lesson is to jump over a very simple, very small upright fence on a slight angle. This should be jumped from both directions and on both angles, left to right and right to left, each way. The jump should be approached at trot, in a good working pace. To be successful and easy to ride in competition, the horse must learn *now* that he remains on a perfectly straight line both on approach and landing, and in mid-air. He must not turn or swing from his line to be at right angles to the fence, but must stay absolutely on the line he is being ridden along and jump precisely where he is asked. Initially, most horses will try to run along the fence a little one way or the other, but with the rider correcting him the

youngster will very quickly get the message and realise that he can jump on an angle. When my horse is happy on a slight angle from every possible direction then I will increase it, at first only a little but then gradually more and more, until we are jumping on really quite an acute angle. And then we can play at angled combination fences.

Once the horse is confident and remaining totally straight when he is presented at any angled jump, we can start to ask him to cope with two jumps like this. The first double I would ask him to do would be two fences, parallel to one another but not in line, placed so that if we jump from centre to centre of them we have 21ft between them. This is grid distance and can therefore be approached slowly in trot, which should make it far easier for the rider to ensure that the horse does remain straight throughout the whole exercise. Again this should be jumped from both directions, so that our horse has to cope with the two different angles. If we want to, with these two fences it is easy to move them to a slightly different place and increase the angle, but care must be taken to keep a correct distance in the centre. If the distance were wrong the horse would really have no option but to run out, and it would be very foolish to destroy his trust and obedience like that.

Once he has jumped parallel fences on an angle I would teach him the other way these jumps can be placed: in line with one another, but not parallel. The second jump can be put at a tangent to the first, so that they are closer together on one side than the other. The distance from centre to centre will again be 21ft, and placed like this the horse will have to cope with a left to right angle on the first and right to left on the second, or vice versa. More tricky for him to work out this time, but providing he does not rush and remains straight, which he should do if his earlier lessons have been learnt correctly, it should present no great problem. Again, this in-and-out should be jumped from both directions.

These exercises can be returned to at any stage in the horse's career, either to remind him that he can jump angles, or to correct a fault which may have appeared, or even as a grid-type exercise to improve his jump. Any number of fences can be jumped at different angles, but the distance should be the same for one non-jumping stride between them. If we were cantering later on then it could be lengthened to 24ft, but generally it is preferable to learn and practise over slightly short distances.

Angles The first time he is presented to a little fence on an angle (1) the young horse has straightened himself up, despite the rider trying to keep him on the required line with an open left rein, but by next time (2) he has got the message well and is staying on a good angle at the centre of the fence.

From the other direction he looks more confident all the way (3 & 4).

3 & 4

Angled combination Two fences on an angle are not so easy, and here (1) the horse is hardly jumping the first at all as he looks at the second, but he keeps the line well and makes a good second jump (2).

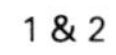

1

3

Corner Fences

Another sort of angle fence is a corner. Any jump which involves two fences which are on an angle and come together – either into a corner or to cross over each other – and can therefore both be jumped over in one effort, needs the same basic approach. The angle created by the two elements of the fence should be bisected in the rider's mind, and then an imaginary line exactly half way between the two elements visualised. The horse should then be presented on a straight approach to this imaginary line, in a place on the fence where both elements can easily be jumped at once. Now the reason for all the insistance on the earlier lessons becomes apparent. It is absolutely imperative that the horse stays totally straight and listens to and trusts his rider. If he drifts to one side he will either run out or, horror of horrors, jump into the second element. To ensure absolutely that there is no possible chance of doing this, the rider should

Corners Here, the horse (Penny) is slightly unsure of our small practice corner (1) and has looked down into the spread and 'backed off' the fence a little too much, but when brought back the other way (2) she is already more confident and is jumping well. When the fence is widened she has learnt well and is quite unconcerned (3) over the now relatively wide corner.

2

always take great care before riding the fence that he is absolutely sure of where to approach and of his line. The fence should be looked at carefully (without the horse, he definitely does *not* want to realise how wide the fence is if he gets it wrong, but must trust his rider and jump where he is told), and once the line is decided the rider should if possible find an object in the background which is on his line so that there is something to aim at. It can be quite difficult without a point to line up on to get the right approach.

I always build my first corner jump in the school from three show jumping uprights and four poles, and initially have a very small jump with one upright at one end and two at the other. We will start with very little width at the double end and just trot to the fence. Even at advanced level a corner is generally not as wide as an ordinary parallel, and it is up to the rider to think of it as just another spread fence which we are approaching exactly where we want to jump it. The rider must never allow himself to look further along the fence and think how wide it is there, but must look up and ride the jump calmly and as well as he would any other obstacle. I like to jump this small corner several times from one direction and then come into it from the other way, so that my horse has learnt about both left-handed and right-handed corners. The width can then easily be increased by moving the two uprights at the wide end farther apart, and in this way we can practise any standard of corner both in trot or canter.

At home we have several corner fences outside. Two are open-type obstacles with various options and routes to jump through them built of post and rails, and one or two are corners created by a rail angled over a ditch. Riders are often horrified and worried by these types of angled fences, but whether the corner or cross is created by normal timber or by a ditch or natural obstacle, the principle is still the same: the angle created must be bisected and the imaginary line between the two elements approached straight – then ditch and rail are easily jumped in one. As with jumping any ditch, the rider must ignore the fact that it is there beneath the fence. He must look up and beyond to the landing, and concentrate on keeping on the correct line and not allowing the horse to straighten up to the rail and therefore jump into the ditch. The more different corner and angle fences jumped, the better for the horse's experience, but the best way to teach and remind him how to do them is with ordinary jumps in a schooling area, and he will then become clever and confident on all sorts of different lines.

(pages 112-13)
A difficult corner Halloween Time shows how a horse who has learnt to jump a corner well can make it look quite easy, even over a fairly complicated fence.

Curves

After learning always to keep straight when approaching fences, either on an angle or at 90° to the centre, then we can teach our horse to approach and jump a fence on a curve, turning all the way. There is really no contradiction here from his earlier lessons: we are continuing to tell him that having put him on any approach or line, whether straight or now curved, his job is to stay on this line and not deviate from or alter it until he is told to do so by his rider.

Just as in his flat work schooling, it should be no great problem to keep him turning around the circle. We will put up two pairs of uprights, both on a circle and probably about 13-14yd – a short three strides – from one another, and then just trot around the circle on both reins without any jumps. One fence will then be constructed at about 2ft high, and we will trot into that and jump in on our circle. On landing the horse will at first probably want to carry on straight, but the rider must bring him back to the circle and carry on round. Rather than keep jumping every time now that we have a fence on the track, I would probably continue for at least half of the circle and then go large, returning to the circle and the jump the next time round.

When the horse is quite happily staying on the circle in the air and on landing we will change the rein, and when both reins are good we will put in a second jump on the other pair of uprights. It is important now to keep thinking of riding around the circle all the time, turning continuously, as we do not want the horse to fall in and straighten between the fences as he did with his previous lesson, but to keep out on a continuous curve. He needs to be able to do this, as sometimes on a cross-country course the nicest route through a combination will often be one with a curving line between two elements, either to get a good distance between the two, or sometimes so that we can be turning back again on landing. If our horse can jump on any angle and keep on any line, whether straight or curved, from both directions, he is going to be a pleasure to ride in competition.

Bounces

'Bounce' fences are another lesson to learn in the school. For the first session we put the pairs of uprights at a distance of about 12ft apart – possibly a little shorter, but no less than 10ft, for a small or small striding horse. We put rails in on the first pair of uprights, and trot over a small jump from both directions, Then a second jump is added on the other pair of uprights, and we come in again in trot. A strong yet not fast trot is needed, rather like riding to a coffin fence.

1

The pen The slightly more experienced horse is now presented with a new pen to jump through on an angle, and while staying totally straight (1) is looking ahead as he jumps in and is assessing what is in front of him. In the air (2) he is already steadying himself, and shortens his stride through the middle (3) to put himself

3

2

right to take off and jump out beautifully (4) over the second element. Throughout the sequence this horse's face shows how much he is thinking for himself while trusting his rider – this is what we want.

4

Bounces are difficult for the horse, as he can only see exactly what he has to do at the last moment. Several strides away a bounce fence will look very like a single spread fence – a wide parallel. The horse may well want to pull on and rush to the fence now, and the rider must not allow him to accelerate but must keep him up together and active behind – he has to jump two fences in quick succession and cannot do that if he has left his back end behind. In the last two or three strides the problem will suddenly look like a trap – like too wide a parallel that cannot be cleared – and the horse must be kept active and balanced and continuing on his approach, and at the last moment he will see that he has room to land and take off again. It is very important for the rider *not* to flop in front of the horse's movement, because immediately he lands he has to be taking off again, and a rider who has his weight on the horse's neck will make this very difficult for him. The rider must try to keep his leg on and his weight behind in order to give the horse the best help to propel himself into the air again.

A bounce is similar again to a coffin-type fence, in that often at the first attempt a young horse will be so busy looking at the second fence that he will make an untidy jump over the first – I have actually trotted *through* the first fence sometimes. Once he has worked out what he has to do – and with no room for a non-jumping stride he will quickly realise that he has to take off again – and he is jumping the bounce nicely, then I will make a different one for him to sort out by changing the rein and coming in from the other direction, sometimes adding another pole to make the second jump a spread.

When my horse is cantering fences we can tackle a bounce in canter. The distance for a height of about 3ft to 3ft 3in wants to be lengthened for canter. The correct distance for a bounce approached in canter outside would be 15ft between the two fences, but indoors I would have about 14ft. Once we are confident in the school, then we can go and tackle a bounce outside which should be no problem.

Rails can also be put at bounce distances both before and after natural fences, such as ditches and banks. The only thing to remember here is that a horse will not jump so far out from these fences, and so to be correct the distance will have to be shortend considerably. A rail on top of a bank to be jumped without a stride on landing will need to be 9ft from the edge of the bank, and that would be the distance I would place a schooling rail after a small ditch.

Upright Fences

One type of fence I always dislike is a gate. This simple-looking jump has tripped up so many horses at all levels: in several different years Burghley three-day event has had a gate which has caused many falls (Delphy Kingfisher and Clarissa Strachan in 1978), and to fall over what is really a solid, rather small show jump at this level is quite ridiculous – and yet it does happen.

If the young horse has been schooled correctly over his show jumps he should learn to jump upright fences like this quite easily and carefully, and when they are met across country the rider should remember to get straight and not go too fast. At speed it is only too easy for the horse to get wrong at the fence, think it is a silly, flimsy-looking jump, hit it hard and trip up, so the rider must approach in a balanced pace with not too much speed so that he can jump accurately and carefully.

Hayracks with a false groundline are similar 'trip-up' fences and again need treating with caution; it is always worth jumping these types of obstacles rather as if they were show jumps. At any level, even when I am trying to go really fast and win, I would prefer to waste a few seconds and have a good jump than to end up with a silly fall – at the least very expensive on the score board, and at worst extremely frightening or damaging to my horse.

Once all the basic types of cross-country fences, both natural and timber, have been schooled over, other combination fences which incorporate several different problems should not really be too difficult to cope with, providing the rider remembers the basic principles of each type of jump. Take, for example, a sunken road. We have a coffin-type rail before the road – approached in a strong, bouncy pace, with just room to land before dropping down into the road – so the horse has to jump out and down as he does off a bank. Then the jump out of the road – we want to get close and jump up exactly as we would onto a bank. Then finally a rail to jump after the road – probably a bounce, so lots of impulsion is needed and the rider must be slightly behind the horse with the leg on, as with a Normandy Bank, so that he can power up and jump again.

Really there are not many new fences to find, just new variations and combinations of tried and tested fences, and if the event horse has a natural aptitude for travelling across country, is taught not to be afraid of new places, and learns how to think about and cope with the basic type of fences he may encounter when he is young, he has really been given the best possible start with lots of simple, easy lessons.

2

First bounce Radjel and myself many years ago. (1) Here we have a horse who is obviously looking ahead to the second fence and is not really concentrating at all on the first. His front legs are therefore typically untidy, and although he jumps cleanly he is still cautious, and is having to be urged forward quite strongly. In the air (2) he looks rather long and disengaged behind, but is still looking towards the second fence and working it all out, and on the landing/take off moment in the

4

1

centre (3) is sorting out which foot goes where quite well. As he jumps again (4) he has really done pretty well for a first attempt, and although he is 'reaching' rather for the fence and looks a bit long and floppy in the air, he has kept quite a good style. The rider has lost her lower leg position as she has had to push, but the body position is not too bad.

3

1

2

3

Bounce with spread By the later attempt with an added spread pole, Radjel looks far more confident. His first jump (1) is much more punchy-looking and round, and his legs are far neater. On landing (2) he is still very good behind and is looking towards the next fence where (3) he puts in a good, confident jump. The rider's lower leg has, hopefully, improved over the years!

5 · EARLY COMPETITIONS

Once my young horse is happily jumping different fences and small courses he is ready to tackle problems away from home – and to go to his first competitions. With several older horses to ride and compete on as well my time tends to be fairly restricted, and *when* I have the time to concentrate on my youngster's career tends to dictate what type of event we go to. If it is autumn, then we have the local hunter trial season and the restricted novice classes can be great fun; if it is winter, then it is unaffiliated indoor show time, and in summer we can track down the riding club shows and events. The type of competition we go to is not as important to me as the standard – I want to find a well built, but tiny size course. Too many young horses are frightened by being asked too much too soon, and I am always prepared not to compete but merely ride around in company and then go home again if I feel that the questions asked are too demanding for the first time. It is quite normal for a young horse to feel far more backward when he is in strange surroundings than he feels at home, and he will often regress several weeks in the presence of strange company.

A dressage show can be the answer for a youngster's initial outing. Our local riding club often has shows where the tests are nice and simple, but I have found that actually managing to steer around the inside of the boards on an excited newcomer can be interesting in itself! Quite often these little shows will have baby-sized clear round jumping and combined training, which is ideal.

Loading

First, though, before we go out to a 'party' we must make sure that we can load easily into the lorry – often a problem with young horses. A few days before the competition we get the lorry out and practise loading when we know we have enough time. Over the years, from landrover and trailer days to our old Bedford TK lorry and on to our super, large six-horse truck today, we have found that bothering to put the time aside to get properly set up and have a loading lesson is well worthwhile. If my horse is quite unconcerned about loading that is great, but if he has a fit and hates the idea the problem can then be sorted out over the next few days at home, and not in the middle of a field at the competition or at home on the big day with every minute ticking by to the start of the show.

We position the lorry so that one side of the ramp is as close as possible to the solid wall of one of the yard buildings. We open up several partitions so that the area he has to go into in the lorry is as large, open and light as possible. A dark, pokey-looking hole is not going to be very encouraging, and too small an area will make the idea of rushing back out again once he is inside far too appealing – when my horse goes up into the lorry I want to make sure he stays there until *I* say he can come out. I make sure we have at least three competent people on hand, as well as an older horse or pony who is a guaranteed loader to act as schoolmaster for the youngster to follow. A bowl with a few nuts as encouragement is also to hand, as are two lungeing whips.

I dress my young horse as if he is actually going to travel, with good protective travelling boots and kneecaps in case he slips going up or down the ramp, but no rugs on him as he will be moving enough to keep warm. I leave his headcollar on, but put his bridle on top. The reins I remove, and use a lunge line fastened on the right side of the bit and threaded through the left to lead him from. The normal headcollar lead rope we put in his partition in the lorry, so that if I do decide to leave him alone, properly tied up as if he were travelling, I can remove his bridle and do so.

We then bring both horses around to the lorry, with the schoolmaster walking in front. We let the youngster stand as close as possible and try to encourage him to watch as his friend climbs up the ramp and disappears into the lorry. The schoolmaster then turns around and comes out, and we get in position for our novice to follow next time. Up the first horse goes, and we shut the partition and leave him in there. Then I lead the young one forward, with one person standing at the open side of the ramp with a lunge whip in the hand nearest the horse and farthest away from the lorry, so that they and the whip are forming a wing or wall to keep him straight. My other helper moves up quietly behind and has the other lunge whip, so that if necessary she can encourage him forward but still keep herself out of reach of his back legs.

Gently but firmly we try to persuade him to keep moving forward to join his friend. My job when leading him is not to try to pull him up the ramp, but to keep him straight and not allow him to turn away. I try to encourage him with my voice to follow me, and the others on the ground should be vocally urging him forward as well. If he hesitates for long then a little flick with the side whip can help, but to hit too hard initially is not a good idea – the idea is to be firm and to give him confidence. If he still resists, then a good hard single crack on his bottom can remind him we do mean business, but before I hit him I make sure that we are all ready, as it will almost certainly cause an explosion of temper, and we do not want to let him charge off but rather keep him there in front of the ramp. Having been beastly to him and told him our meaning we then keep niggling and encouraging as before. Offering him the nuts can help, but often this simply makes too many things for the leader to hold. By firmly being good guys and nasty guys in this way, I have found that the horse will usually clamber up the ramp to join his friend in safety pretty quickly.

1

Loading (1) Our youngster is positioned so that he can see his schoolmaster going up the lorry ramp, and looks a little apprehensive as he watches. But by the time it is his turn (2) he drops his head and looks, and with encouragement (3) decides to go up and into the lorry.
Unloading Once the horse is quite happy and relaxed inside the lorry, out he comes – carefully (4) – and we practice again.

2

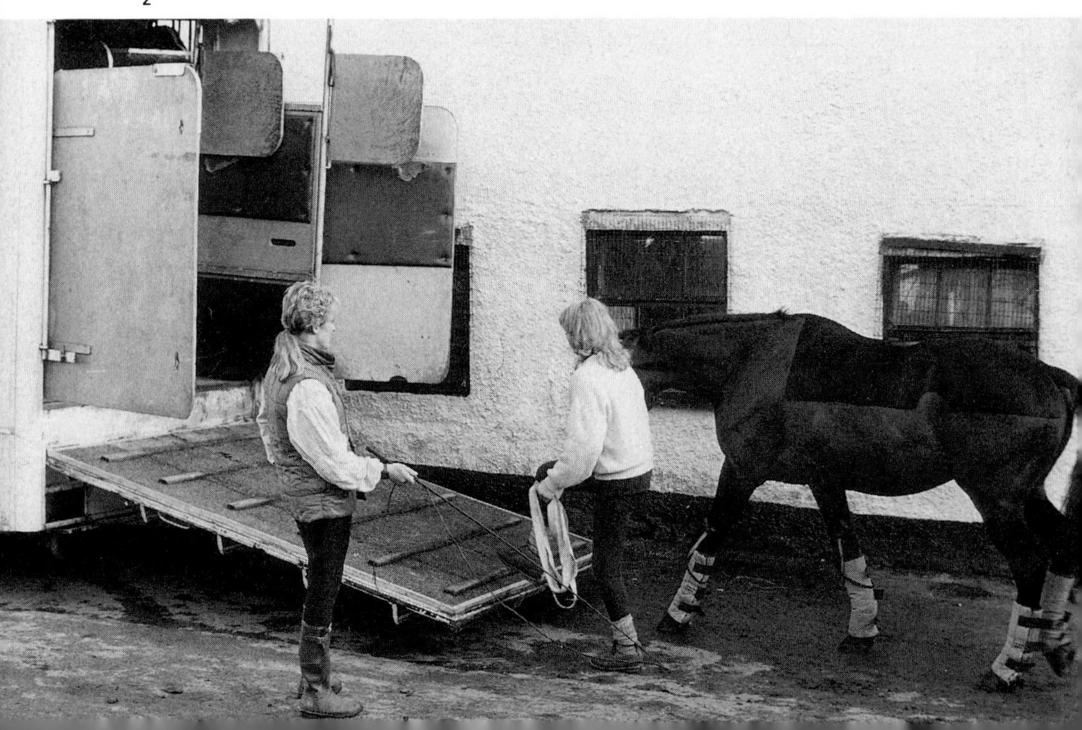

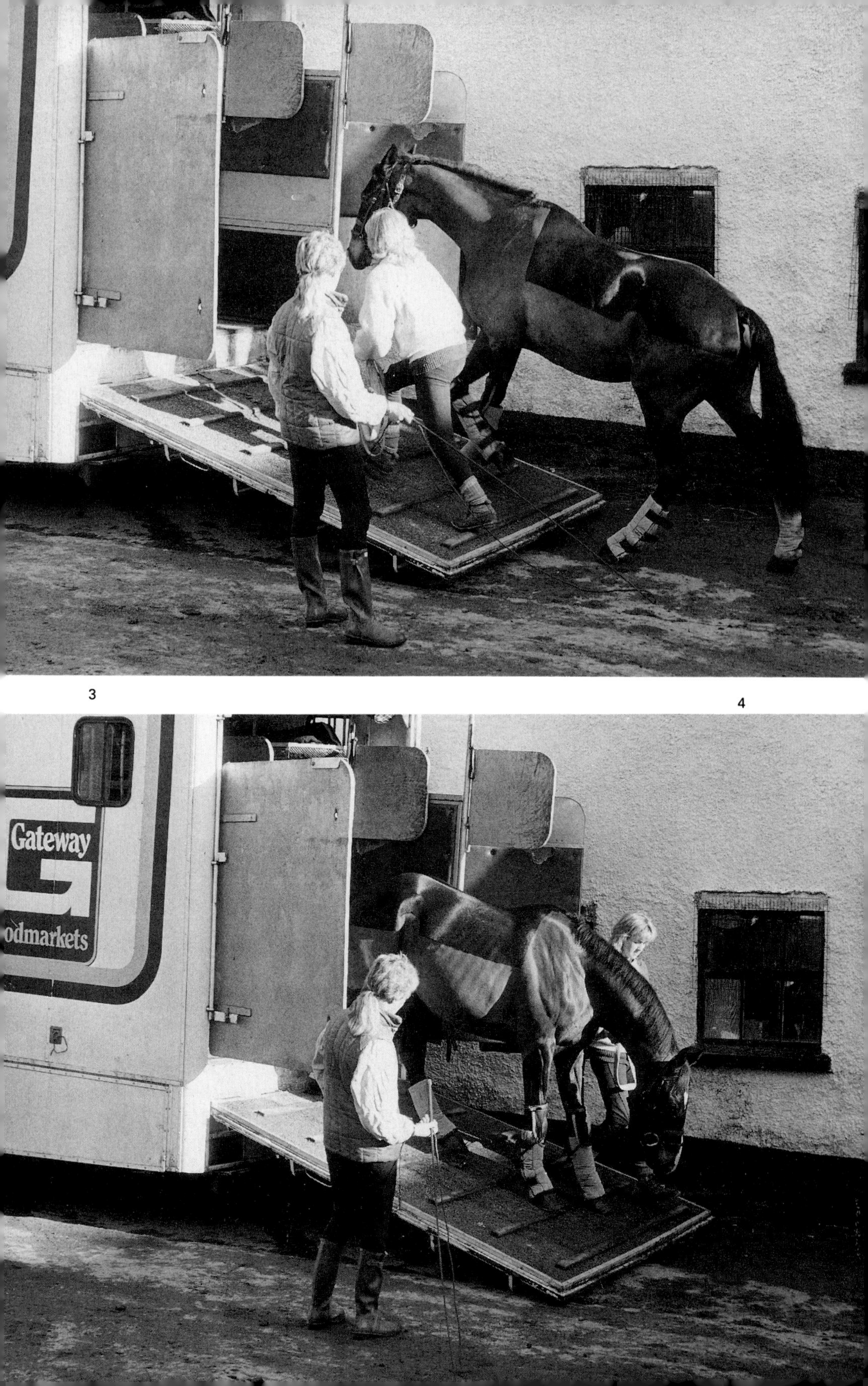
3
4
Gateway
odmarkets

If he is being really difficult, we just keep on trying until he gives up. The great advantage of having a lunge line on the bridle is that I can play my horse like a fish if he does try to whip around and run away. I hate to leave the ramp myself, feeling that if I start running around with the horse to re-position him then he is exerting his will over me. I try to stay where I am, and let the others push him back to square one if he tries to turn away. I am not a great fan of a lunge line or rope behind young horses to pull them in; although this method can work brilliantly, particularly with naughty ponies, I have found that characterful, scopey horses tend to realise very quickly that if they stand up and rear, and swing around as they do so, then they can drop their front legs over the rein or rope and beat us, as we have to stop, extract the rope and start again.

Once the horse does give in and climb into the lorry then lots of praise is needed. I like to shut the partition, let him speak to his friend and tell him how difficult it was, give them both some nuts and leave them to settle in the lorry.

Our lesson for the day does not stop here though. When the youngster has settled, we open the partition and let him walk out, and then turn and walk back in. This is almost the most important part of the whole lesson: that loading in and out of the lorry is something that is done to command whenever, and however often, he is asked. It is nothing to be afraid of, but just a normal procedure and not a 'one off'. Loading away from home will be more difficult, so we wait to be sure that in our own surroundings we can go in and out as we want. So it is back in again, and however long it takes it is never as time-consuming as the first time. Same procedure, then out again, and we keep going in and out until he is quite unworried by the whole thing and I hardly need my helpers. *Then* the lesson is over for the day. Depending on how much, if any, of a battle we may have had, we may well repeat the lesson again on one or two more days. I do not want any hassle on our first competition morning before we even start.

The First Competition

So the big day dawns and my horse's competition career is about to begin. If at all possible I try to take along an older horse as company for him, even if he is not taking part in the event. To his delight, Merry Sovereign (now retired at the age of twenty-one) has been enlisted for this job several times, and thinks it is marvellous fun to be at a party again. A helper to assist with tacking up, loading, practice jumps etc is essential for the first few outings – I usually find that all equine manners seem to disappear in the excitement of the first few events.

Walking the Course

At whatever level I am competing across country I prefer if possible to walk the course the day before. Invariably time has a tendency to become limited on the day of the competition, and it is far easier not to have to worry about when you are going to fit in walking the course. If you do walk on the day, an hour and a half is really needed at a one-day event between phases or before the dressage; if it is only a cross-country competition or hunter trial I would allow myself this long from arriving to being 'on horse' if I had to walk the course. To be hurried usually results in either a rushed decision about where to jump a fence, or an ill-prepared or incorrectly tacked up horse – and all the months of careful preparation are wasted. With a complicated course another great advantage of walking the day before is that it does still allow time to either re-walk the whole course the following day if necessary, or to return to any fences I am not quite sure about for a second look.

My advice to any novice rider is to try to walk the course with an experienced rider, if possible your trainer or teacher. The 'experienced eye' will often spot a problem (or easy route) that will have totally escaped the nervous or excited novice, and can make the difference between a clear round and disaster. If your trainer is not going to be there, then try to find a seasoned competitor whom you know to walk with, and if that is not possible be brave and go and ask someone who you do not actually know personally, but whose judgement you respect, for their advice with any worries you may have. We international riders are not fierce and are quite happy to try to help – I only wish that people would ask me for advice more often.

So, when we walk the course what are we looking for? I like to look ahead to the fence coming and observe the lie of the land: are we approaching uphill or down, or even across the camber of the hill? Uphill may tire the horse, but even young horses do seem to find it quite easy to jump uphill – their hocks come up under them naturally on the slope and give them extra activity – whereas downhill it is usually more difficult to be balanced. The running away and gaining speed tendency downhill will make a young horse back off and check himself, usually resulting in an unbalanced feeling and often in slipping and sliding. The hindquarters almost seem to disconnect, and more effort has to be made by the rider on a downhill approach to re-balance before the last few strides to the fence. Going across the camber is always a problem. The young horse will try to straighten his ground, and always seems to prefer to adjust himself to going up the hill rather than across it, so great attention has to be paid to maintaining the desired line to the fence.

Also as I approach I try to see if the obstacle looks spooky or odd in any way – my horse is going to be moving faster than I am, and I want to be ready for him if he does see something funny in the fence. Another thing to watch on the approach is how the landing and getaway looks. If there is a sharp turn after the jump, or a dark wood or lane to enter, it could well influence my horse. He may feel there is no way for him to go when he lands, and may quite logically decide that it is therefore safer and more sensible *not* to jump the fence and get himself into trouble. So if this problem is evident, I must be ready for his reaction.

Always try to look forward to the fence as you walk towards it and decide before the last three strides how it looks. Does it seem an easy, straightforward fence, or does it look as if it has a hidden problem lurking behind it? Some fences will appear easier in the last few strides and some more difficult and your riding must allow for this, as must your horse's pace. Any obstacle which is basically a 'fly' or galloping single fence but has a ditch either beneath, in front or behind it must be attacked firmly, even in the early days of trotting over mini obstacles – once these sorts of jumps have been refused they are not at all easy to jump second time. The horse should never look into the ditch at all, and we must keep his eye on the top of the fence so that he jumps exactly what he sees three strides away: a straightforward, going-on fence, If he learns to look into the depths of the ditches under these fences we will never succeed.

Jumps with hidden problems after them – such as coffins, water to land in or cross, drops and even combinations – need riding very differently, as in these cases my horse must be allowed time to see what he has to cope with on landing, and realise that it is safe to go. With these sorts of problems he does not want to leap over bravely without looking and land in trouble, so as you walk round you must assess what speed and how much impulsion you will need. Generally speaking, this type of jump becomes far clearer in the last three strides, so you must ride accordingly and make sure that as you take off the problem is already half solved.

As you walk on around the course it is important to note the actual terrain and length of the course. Is it a long, tiring course or one that is comparatively undemanding on my horse's fitness? A young horse will not be as fit as an older one, and must be 'nursed along' if he has a lot to do. We will not be in a hurry, so where there are good open stretches of ground we can slow down and amble along if the youngster does tire. As with all the training at home, it is vital that he finishes by thinking it was easy and *fun* – and we must make sure that it is.

That thought has to be foremost in your mind when you are deciding where to go at combinations and alternatives. Although we want our horse to learn at the baby level how to jump bounces, corners and angles, we must also be absolutely sure in our minds that he is ready for any question we ask him. For his first few competitions we will tend always to go the easier way, and concentrate on how he copes: does he stay straight, is he bold, does he listen? Then in the future we will know how he will react and how to ride him as we start to tackle the more difficult routes. But still, at whatever level, and however much you may want to win, the golden rule is only to take on ways that you know are no problem for your horse and your riding. There are no extra prizes for having jumped all the 'big' ways – clear rounds are what count.

Preparation

It is a great help if a young horse has been to a few shows as an unbroken baby to be shown in hand, but mine have usually been complete novices at public functions when I start with them. I like to have my schoolmaster in the lorry first, with the youngster next to him and as far into the lorry as possible so that we can open up the partitions as much as we can and tack up inside the lorry the first time. With the adrenalin pumping, it can be extremely difficult to persuade a big horse to allow a bridle to go on outside when he is peering around like a giraffe at everything or, worse, trying to dash off and join in the fun and games, and standing still for a saddle can be equally impossible. I usually put a set of brushing boots and a pair of overreach boots on at home underneath the travelling boots, so that all we have to do to their legs is take off the top layer. I get myself dressed ready to go – number included, as that can be fun to put on when sitting on an excited time bomb – then out he comes and on I get.

Riding-in

Once I am safely on board I have to try to ride my horse in a little without losing control – not easy, unless there is a good practice area. If we are near to quiet roads then I may disappear for twenty minutes' quiet hacking, but if that is not possible then we have to join the other horses. I often feel at indoor shows that this is the hardest part of early competitions – actually getting to the ring. At unaffiliated shows and hunter trials there are often masses of small ponies charging around, which is very exciting for the youngster. Unfortunately, most of their riders seem to think that large adults on big horses are totally in control, whereas we are usually far less in command than they are. Many times I have had a young horse who has either fallen in love with a small pony and tried to follow it everywhere or, worse, decided to be terrified of one and run away in the opposite direction – both equally embarrassing.

I am not over-concerned with how long I ride in for. If it is really difficult to get any concentration, then I would rather go straight on and do my bit in the ring or on the course, where at least I should be able to settle him as we perform alone. With all the excitement and moving around when loading and travelling and on arrival, he is probably pretty well warmed up already – unlike the old hands who sleep all the way to the events – and I prefer to get on with it and let him do his bit.

If we are at a hunter trial then I try to avoid any queuing system, and if the starting steward insists on having his next twenty competitors actually standing waiting then I get my ever-willing helper to queue for me. If we can find a small practice fence then I will trot over it two or three times when there are about six more starters to go before me, and then just try to walk quietly around and wait my turn. If there were *masses* to go before me I have occasionally re-boxed my horse and waited until nearer our turn to start again – it is never a bad thing on arrival at a hunter trial to look at the starter's board and assess when to start working in, so that the perils of hanging around for hours on an over-excited youngster can be avoided.

Riding the Course

Once we start I go slowly, and just trot the first few fences, even if there is a 'timed section'. The object of the exercise today is to gain experience and learn, not to win. Anyway, with the inevitably large number of starters the class will invariably be won by a small speed merchant pony and expert child; I think the times that I have been placed in a hunter trial could be counted on one hand. If a fence is straightforward with a good approach I may canter to it, but I am quite happy to canter on between the jumps and drop back to trot to allow my horse to assess the problem (and myself more control in steering) on the approach to each obstacle. I try to keep a careful ear open for faster competitors about to overtake me. If they are coming I am quite happy to circle away and trot about by myself, and then re-commence when they have gone and we have a free run once more.

Hopefully, my horse will gain confidence with every fence, and by the end will really be enjoying himself and looking forward to what is coming next. If there is another class at the same height or slightly bigger, then we can go once more later: to do the same course or similar again, providing it did not take too much out of him the first time, can only build up confidence as he should find it easy this time, and with any luck he will go home thinking what a clever fellow he is because this game is easy.

Other Classes

If we go to an indoor or outdoor baby jumping show, then I follow the same procedure for timing my young horse's entrance into the collecting ring: start early enough to have coped with the traumas of tacking up, but not with so much time that once he is out he can start to think of silly games. I will try to settle him on the flat – often *very* difficult and exciting as other horses jump the practice jump and whizz around – and then get my helper to make the practice fence into a small cross pole. I would only ever trot the practice fence at this stage in his career: our competition will be easily jumpable in trot, and we will canter another day. Once I am happy with how he is hopping over this we will put up a small upright fence, and then progress on to a little parallel. When that is satisfactory, off we go to the ring.

I always try my hardest to ensure that my horse's first jumping class will be clear round jumping. Then if we do have horrible problems about going near strange fences I should be able to have several attempts, and win the battle. I will pay for three rounds and ask if I may jump them consecutively: hopefully, two is all we will need, but I like to have the third kept like a rabbit in a hat, ready to pull out if needed. In we go and trot slowly around. As when we were schooling, I try very hard to be ready for any spooking and keep behind him, particularly at the doubles. Once we have negotiated our first round, however well or badly, then I carry straight on and repeat the exercise. Ninety per cent of the time this second effort will be fine, but if he *is* naughty out comes the rabbit turn, and we go again. Lots and lots of praise is given when he has been good, and back he goes into the lorry. If there is a novice class at similar heights then we will stay and jump once more; if not, then home we go. In the fairly unlikely event of jumping a clear round in the class, then of course we do not go any faster in the jump off – that comes a lot later.

Further Competitions

Once we start competing I like to keep going as regularly as possible. My ideal schedule with a new young horse would be to go to our first outing in late summer, if possible to a small riding club show, with perhaps a baby dressage class but *certainly* with clear round jumping. I would aim to do three or four of this type of show, by which time the hunter trial season would be starting. As the first course we take on is important, I would make quite sure that it was suitable right at the start. Hopefully we should manage to find several hunter trials and, if we are lucky, a small one-day

event. When I had Chatsby as a four-year-old he did a marvellous baby-size proper one-day event, and became a proven event horse at a very tender age. Then, when the outdoor season finishes I will jump indoors throughout the winter and should, all being well, progress through the unaffiliated classes to official BSJA competitions. Ideally, when the weather improves again in the spring I would try to find one or two outside competitions and, if all is going well, on to a pre-novice BHS event and then to the real thing, novice BHS events, and his career proper is under way.

By now, of course, I am experienced enough in producing youngsters to go this quickly if I have a talented horse, but my most earnest advice to others (and to myself) is *do not* be tempted to hurry. Harm is far easier to do than to undo. A guideline question I always keep in mind is 'How do I expect my horse to go in the competition?' I should feel that he will either go clear, or possibly make one or two mistakes. Any worse and he is not ready – being delighted to 'get round' is invariably the first step to a frightened, overfaced horse in the future. If he finds each step up the ladder comparatively easy, he will then look forward to every new challenge.

Quite early on in his career, Radjel makes a big fence at Locko Park, in the 1981 National Championships, feel quite small. Before he came to me he had done a lot of show jumping, which made him very confident of jumping a big fence.

6 · FITNESS AND FEEDING

Once we have decided that the horse is ready to commence his BHS eventing career, it is time to start thinking seriously about his fitness. Having a horse fit enough to cope easily with every level of eventing is just about the most important part of all the training. Too many horses are spoilt by being taken out and asked to run when they are not physically ready – if the body is not fit, strain of some sort is the only answer to the stress they will be under, and a bad strain can end a horse's career before it ever begins. Even a minor strain will mean weeks or maybe months off the road recovering, followed by weeks of slow work building back up again, and it will always leave at best a worry, and at worst a weakness. Asking a tired horse to gallop and jump is also foolish, and potentially dangerous. The tired horse will be far more likely to make mistakes in judgement, and could badly injure himself and/or his rider if he does. He will also finish feeling awful, and if he has any sense he will realise very quickly that cross-country is not a nice experience at all and will start to stop. So the weeks of slow fitness preparation must never be neglected, and will pay dividends with a sound, happy horse for years in the future.

We are very lucky living where we do. Our farm is in the bottom of a valley so we have enough flat fields for our canter and gallop work, and yet there are miles of huge hills behind the farm where we can do our road-work on the small country roads. Our only snag is having to do a mile either over the fields (trying not to get bucked off in winter) or on a very busy main road (the horses which are good in traffic are invaluable here) to get to the lanes. Still, I think we have as good facilities as any.

Creating a Fitness Programme

My young horse will carry on to his first proper event – generally the pre-Novice class – from his unaffiliated events and jumping shows. He will usually have built up to jumping BSJA Newcomers or even Foxhunter, so will already be fit enough to do an hour to an hour and a half of mixed work. About six weeks before my first event I look ahead and map out a programme on a calendar or in my diary. My advice to any rider working towards their first event season is to get either their trainer or a local experienced event rider to sit down with them and help them work out how much work to do and when – and then stick to the schedule.

(pp138-9) Merry Sovereign and I just before the dressage at Luhmuhlen Three-Day Event. Sovereign was a superb horse in the dressage, but never easy to ride or time just right in the arena – he was no problem to produce at peak fitness but persuading him then to be good and obedient in the dressage was quite tricky. Despite my worried look (and his naughty one) he was super that day.

MASTER FIDDLER: One of the biggest fences over a ditch that there is, the Badminton Parallel Bars, and Fiddler is putting in a big, brave jump to find it no real problem

21

DELPHY DAZZLE: (left) Super confidence over a nasty drop combination and (above) the same confidence and total trust over the notorious fourth fence in the Burghley European Championships – a horrid obstacle that he made feel easy

DELPHY KINGFISHER: Really stretching out over the Badminton Horsens Bridge, an enormous-looking fence that, if tackled bravely like this, is not as bad as it looks

Roadwork

In the final six weeks before the first event we do an hour and a half on the roads every day, just walking – briskly, not ambling along. Remember that a horse can wander around the field all day and never get fit, so he must be made to work and walk out properly, with trotting just up the hills.

I am convinced that long, slow work on the roads is extremely important in hardening up the legs and producing a fit horse. When you look at trainers of National Hunt (hurdle and steeplechase) horses – the nearest equivalent to the event horse for fitness demands – and event horses, the ones with a consistently successful soundness record with their charges always seem to do a lot of roadwork. Too much trotting will only produce jarring and do harm, so we only trot up two or three big hills per ride – but some of our hills have a rise of approximately seven hundred feet in about half a mile, so they do have to work! If we are short of riders or time we will sometimes ride one horse and lead another, but I do not feel the led horse does quite as much work as the ridden one. For this reason I try to ride and then lead on alternate days, and to do a slightly longer ride to make sure the led horse does enough. Here this can work very well, with the advanced horses, who need a little more work, leading the novices.

Our regular routine is to brush the horse off before exercise and then either groom well or wash off on return to the stables. If the horse is totally dry and has not really sweated at all then he can be well brushed to remove any dirt, then rugged up and put away, but if he has worked hard and is either still wet and sweaty or even just a little sticky the only way to ensure he will not 'break out' into a cold, clammy sweat again is to wash him off. Providing this is done as soon as the horse comes back in from work when he is still warm he will not find it chilling – after all, the human athlete goes straight into the shower after a workout – and if all the salty sweat is washed away he will be found to dry off and feel lovely and warm very quickly after being scraped off and re-rugged with a sweat rug underneath. Here, even in the coldest weather, after canter or gallop work the horses are brought in still steaming and warm, and are then taken straight into a washing off bay where they can be hosed off inside out of any draught immediately – and we have never had any problem with cold 'broken out' horses after work.

Rest Days

If my horse is schooled on the flat, his roadwork is not cut down by the time he has schooled: I will school him on top of his roadwork. Bill Noble trains me for dressage and comes to us for a day's work with all us aspiring Devonians, so if we do a full session of an hour's hard work with Bill I

may cut the roadwork time down to a good hour – but I never *replace* the long slow work with the dressage. Similarly, if I jump or canter my horse I may adjust the roadwork a little – but only a little. My horses do not get a day off once a week as a routine; although this may be a good idea, my horses are usually going to indoor (or outdoor in summer) jumping shows at least once a week, and for an event horse the amount of work they do at these is not a lot, so I am afraid this has to count as their day off. If, after an event, they have a day off then they do not just stand in and do nothing. If they are turned out every day then we will turn them out as usual and not ride them at all, and if they do not go out then we take them for a twenty-minute ridden walk. We either ride down to a place nearby where we go in the river and let them play – they learn to love this and splash and dig holes like little children – or we walk a short circuit on the road.

I am very aware of the possibility of azoturia in fit horses. One of the worse things about it is that it is recurrent, and only too often each attack is triggered off more easily and more often. The fit horse who stands in one day and then works hard the next is the horse who is likely to be hit by this 'tieing up' attack, and we are always trying to avoid any creation of the cause of azoturia. For this reason, if our horses do have a day off, either as routine or after an event, we then only walk our normal roadwork on the following day. The next day we trot the hills as usual, and on the third day after the day off return to canter work or jumping or schooling. This may seem over-cautious, but I would far rather be safe than sorry.

Canter Work

The next problem to work out in the fitness programme is *where* to do the canter work. Good ground and going is absolutely essential – cantering or galloping on bad ground is the surest way to strain or damage a horse, either in competition or training, and should be avoided at all costs. A bad strain or even breakdown is so often the end of a horse's career, but steady training on good going should build up a fit hard horse without strains and problems on the way.

The ground to look for should be level, without potholes or poaching from animals in the wet, and ideally firm enough not to cut up badly when worked on, but soft enough to absorb some of the concussion from a large

---

Roadwork Hills like these are a tremendous advantage for training the event horse. Our horses will sweat and blow every day working up these inclines, and are consequently not at all difficult to get fit. Here, both horses are swinging along nicely in trot up the hill and are about to return to walk at the top, having started trotting right down at the bottom in the village.

horse's weight. It should have footprints left to see after it has been worked over, but not cut into at any depth, otherwise by next time the ground will be poached and unlevel. If you have to canter when the ground is very wet, then great care has to be taken to observe when it starts to dry up and then move away from the unlevel ground to a good surface. The abandoned ground can then be harrowed and rolled and allowed to settle and dry out into a level surface once more, ready to be cut up again! When the ground dries right out and becomes very hard, but cannot be avoided, then it is vital *not* to work too fast and to keep to an even pace to avoid damage to the horse. Watering the ground would be marvellous, but with the vast amounts of water needed would not be within most riders' budgets.

Grass, preferably old turf, has to be generally accepted as the best surface for canter and gallop work. To train on the surface that we are going to compete on must make sense, as the horse has then been conditioned to this going and will not have to adjust to a different feel underfoot when he is out. Here at home we are lucky: we use a meadow which is two furlongs (a quarter of a mile) long. It is nice and level and has the river Culm running along it. This is great, as where we canter beside the river seems to drain well in the winter when we have a heavy rainfall, and somehow never dries out quite as much as some of the rest of the land in the summer – the river seems to water it. The only problem with cantering along the banks is wildlife – we have all learnt to sit very tight until we have been along and back once and flushed out the ducks, and many times I have gained speed at all sorts of odd tangents from the riverbank when a panicking duck takes fright and my horse panics in sympathy.

At each end of the meadow we have enough room to do a semi- circle of about forty metres and turn back to the river. This is very useful, and I think better than a circular gallop, as we have to constantly work at the horses' balance and obedience in order to turn correctly. They have to allow themselves to be steadied and come back to a slower pace with an even rhythm, turn correctly with a little bend (listening to the outside rein and leg), and then change legs as they change direction. I do not push for the leg change: rather as with the initial canter strike off on the flat, horses will learn to change in their own time as it becomes more comfortable to do so. I tend to *encourage* the change, but if they want to carry on in counter canter then, so long as they are balanced, I leave them to do so. If a horse is pushed and chased to change, then often he will develop a major hang-up and a conviction that it is impossible to do so – left alone, I have never found a horse who does not change when he has to. Master Fiddler has always been very reluctant to change when cantering at home, and if he feels balanced and rideable in counter canter then that is fine by me.

Yet when I move him on and actually gallop or jump cross-country fences he does the most perfect flying changes, so I never worry about the lack of them in canter work.

How a horse canters is vital. Too many event riders never even think of schooling their horses while training, and it is essential. Jumping fences fast is all about basic training on the flat, and all the basics must be worked on and kept up to scratch as much when working in canter and gallop as with the flat work in the school. The horse should accept a little bend left or right when asked, turn where and when needed, and lengthen and shorten his stride without resistance or loss of rhythm – *then* he will be quick and easy to ride cross country. To do this well he must stay on the bit and carry himself just as he does for his dressage work, and the rider must concentrate and be aware that he is correct in his way of going all the time.

Canter work A good, balanced canter, and although Halloween Time is a little overbent he is still working well and looks as if it would be no problem for him to alter his pace or jump a fence.

When we need to do occasional fast work here we can now lengthen our gallop track. Last year we opened a gap through the hedge into the next field, building a bridge over the existing ditch, and now can go on for another furlong and a half, finishing with an incline of about five hundred yards uphill which 'blows out' their wind beautifully. It is very important constantly to observe the state of the going, and to harrow and roll when necessary. We also try to walk along our track on foot as often as possible and pick up any stones which may have worked up to the surface – a stone landed on at speed can do a lot of damage. The grass keep here is let to a local farmer (an ex point-to-point jockey himself) who grazes cattle and sheep. The sheep particularly are marvellous minders of the going, permanently maintaining a good length of grass, and their little feet help tread in the hoofprints.

Training Grounds

The necessity for good ground is unavoidable for training horses, whether for racing or eventing. If you are lucky enough to have suitable ground of your own, as we are, then life is easier, but if you do not then you have to find it. Even here, we travel when necessary, either because of frosty or extreme wet weather, or occasionally for fast work in the summer when the ground is hard. It is possible to find suitable canter and gallop ground, but (as with many aspects of training horses) it can be hard work. Farmers with a good field can be approached, and are often willing to lend or hire a field for occasional use, and local racehorse trainers who have put down expensive gallops will often be quite happy to hire them out for a fee and have their facilities paying for themselves. To shy away from the expense of travelling to, and even paying for the use of, good ground to work on is one of the most foolish of false economies. Competition horses *are* expensive, and all the time and expense can be written off and wasted in one minute of fast work on bad ground.

If our ground is impossible we have on occasion travelled to a local beach. A bad beach is very dangerous to canter on, and the surface must be 'true' and consistent. We have only two suitable beaches, one (the best) fifty miles away – only an hour by motorway – at Burnham. Canter work *only* is the rule of the day here, as hitting one of the soft patches which are impossible to see would be potentially lethal at speed. Still, if the ground at home is unworkable the fitness programme can be carried on at the beach. Despite the hassle of having to travel I always enjoy the beach, particularly Sandy Bay near Exmouth where we can ride in the waves when we have finished cantering. The horses love this once they have overcome their initial horror of the waves bubbling towards them.

All-weather tracks and surfaces are very useful too – I would love to have one here – but I still prefer good grass going above all. Most of the top racing trainers will try to work their best prospects on grass, so it should be the best for our event horses if we can find it.

Judging Speed

Here, if possible, I work out a programme for cantering my horses for six weeks before the first event. The speed we canter at is 400m per minute, approximately one mile every four minutes. To discover initially how fast to go, the distance worked over must be measured. Either a measuring wheel should be used, or it should be paced by foot (by a proven accurate measurer) or measured with a vehicle's milometer, and then with the use of a stopwatch the correct speed can be gauged. Judging the speed in training is so important, and it is very easy to think that by going slightly faster the horse will become fitter more quickly, but he will not – he will simply be in far more danger of straining himself and will not necessarily build up his body muscles to true fitness. I still use my stopwatch constantly when doing canter work to check and monitor my speed – it is strange how different horses will make the same speed feel totally different.

Carrying out the Programme

Although every horse is different and will train on to fitness in a varied way, in a horse's first season I will follow the same programme every time. Then I can observe whether my young horse is easy to get fit or is one who takes time, and later in his career I can adjust my basic programme a little to suit him best.

The first canter will be for two minutes. just once up and back along our gallop. My programme involves canter work every three days, and our next will be for three minutes. The three day interval is very important, and should never in my opinion be shortened, although it may occasionally be lengthened to four days. It is accepted that the horse needs this time to recover physically from hard work; to work him more frequently will inevitably involve working him when his muscles are still tired, and tired muscles are easy to strain. Each successive canter should push him on a little farther, but not be unduly stressful. I like to think of myself: if I have a pulled or aching muscle and I work it hard the next day, it will feel worse. Use it gently and normally and the next day, it feels better, and I am sure horses are the same. We increase the time spent cantering by approximately one minute every or every other canter until our final one, which comes a week before the event. This canter lasts for eight minutes, therefore covering two miles, and this is slightly longer than our event

Programme for Novice BHS Events

	Monday	Tuesday	Wednesday	Thursday	Friday	Saturday	Sunday
Week 1 1½ hrs roadwork daily	Canter 2 min			Canter 3 min			Canter 3min
Week 2 Roadwork as Week 1			Canter 4 min			Canter 4 min	
Week 3 Roadwork as Week 1			Canter 5 min			Canter 5 min	
Week 4 Roadwork as Week 1		Canter 6 min (possibly substitute fast 4 furlongs)			Canter 6 min		
Week 5 Roadwork as Week 1	Canter 7 min			Canter 7 min (possibly substitute fast 6 furlongs)			Canter 8 min
Week 6 Roadwork as Week 1				Canter 4 min			Novice One-Day Event: 1½ miles
Week 7 Roadwork as Week 1	Day off: 20 min walk	Walking exercise (see p145)	Back to normal roadwork		Canter 4 min		
Week 8 Roadwork as Week 1	Canter 6 min			Canter 4 min			Novice One-Day Event: 1½ miles

which will be about one and a half miles in length. I will canter once more mid-week before the event but drop back to a four-minute canter, which should be enough to work off any excess energy but still leave my horse feeling keen and fresh on the big day.

Building Fitness Through Events

If we have a series of events, which I would always plan to do once my horse has started his career, then his fitness has to be assessed at each one. I would aim to do approximately a dozen events in his first year, preferably with a short break in the middle.

In the first season winning and upgrading, or even gaining points, will not be important, and as we therefore will not be galloping fast across country my youngster will not need to increase his fitness. As a rough guide, I will still canter him every three days – after building up carefully again, of course, if he has had a day off after an event – probably for four to six minutes depending on how fit he feels. If we have two or three weeks without an event we may not canter for a week, then do a six- and then an eight-minute canter, gradually building up again. But every horse has to be assessed individually as to how much he needs. With very fit horses I have sometimes not cantered at all at home if we have had events two weeks apart, but just schooled and kept up the roadwork – the last thing we want is an over-fit horse who becomes difficult to settle and ride.

As the young horse's performance gets more established and professional, he will begin to be ready to be ridden faster and to win some prizes. Very rarely have I done fast work at home with novices – I have usually built up their speed and performance from event to event. If I did have a novice horse I wanted to produce ready to gallop and win in his first event – probably in his second year, if he was still novice grade – then I would substitute fast work for two of his canters. Ten days before the event we would do six furlongs fast, and three canters (nine days) before that four furlongs fast. Fast work, though, should still be on the bit and with a 'gear in hand'. Simply to chase the horse flat out is not the object of the exercise – he should move forward quickly but still very much in balance, and with a little in reserve. Following this system with the roadwork as well should result in a horse suitably fit for novice events – and, hopefully, a sound horse at the end of the season.

Feeding

Feeding the event horse correctly is an important part of his training, and careful attention should be paid to the amount and type of food he eats throughout his career.

With a young horse before he is in work grass is the best natural feed, particularly good grass such as we have here. Our farm in the Culm Valley is very good grazing land, and if we turn the horses out for a break in the best growing months of late spring and early summer you can almost *see* them gaining weight. If an unbroken horse looks well in the summer months grass alone should be enough for him, but when the weather deteriorates and the grass stops growing and loses its goodness then he will almost certainly need some good hay, and possibly a hard feed of concentrates each day. In this case I would give him about 4-6lbs in total, made up probably of 1lb bran and the rest oats, coarse mix and event cubes. We always feed a multi-vitamin supplement to all our horses daily, which ensures that they have a supply of all the vitamins in the correct percentages so that their bodies can take and use what they require, and the young horse out at grass would have this supplement in his feed.

Throughout my horses' careers they are fed a little bran, and then the rest of their hard feed is made up of oats, coarse mix and event cubes. Of course, each horse will vary and have his own preference for a certain type of feed, and we try to discover through careful observation which feedstuffs he eats well and really seems to like. If a definite preference emerges, then we will feed what he likes best in a slightly larger quantity than the other feeds. Dazzle has always had strong likes and dislikes: at one stage in his career he refused to eat cubes at all, whereas last year he decided that coarse mix was quite marvellous. The skill in feeding each horse lies in realising what he likes and dislikes *before* he goes on a hunger strike and refuses to eat at all.

Worming

From the very first day a young horse arrives here he goes onto a strict worming programme, which we follow in accordance with our vet, Mr Attenburrow's, advice. Every six months, and always when a new horse arrives, we take a dung sample which goes to the laboratory at Mr Attenburrow's practice, where they carry out a worm count. If the count is abnormally high, then we can follow a more frequent programme of worming than usual until the count is minimal – and that is what they should all be.

In the past I bought two horses who looked very fit and healthy when they arrived, and we carried on worming them regularly with the others here. After several months they began to look a little thin, and then worse, so we sent off a sample in each case for a worm count. Both times the count was horrifically high – and I was furious with myself, because if they had been checked when they first arrived we would almost certainly have discovered they were a little too high then, put them on a course of wormings at short intervals and kept them looking fat and well. One lives and learns – and all my new arrivals have worm counts done immediately now. On Mr Attenburrow's instructions we worm all the horses every six weeks, using one product – Strongid sachets at the moment – for three times, then another – Eqvalan paste – for one, and then back to the first product again.

Hay

When our young horses come in to be broken the main bulk of their feed is hay – good hay. We used to make and use our own, but now my father lets out the grazing we have to buy all the hay in. Although it is more expensive than our own, at least we can ensure that it is all first class – when you make your own it is often difficult to use up or sell the not so good bales.

My horses seem to prefer to eat, and do better on, a fairly firm mixture of hay, more seed than meadow. Unless we have a very fat and overweight horse, when youngsters are being broken they get as much hay as they want to eat, and not too much hard feed. It is more important that they remain sane and sensible, and therefore safe to handle, than look and feel too good and become unsettled and silly, which can happen very easily with too much hard feed.

We feed our hay soaked, again on our horse doctor's advice, and we have a row of plastic dustbins that we fill with dry hay, top up with water from the hosepipe and leave to soak for twenty-four hours; we then tip up the bins and feed the hay as soon as it has drained. We are also now using a large, self-tipping container which is very easy to operate and soaks a large amount of hay. This removes any dust that is present in the hay and should help the horses' wind – and an event horse is going to need his wind to be in top condition. Drawing a parallel with myself I have found that dry hay causes me tremendous sneezes, and yet soaked hay never does, and many people find exactly the same relief from hay snuffle when working with soaked hay.

A Planned Diet

Every stable, even if it only houses one horse, should have a feed board with the horse's name and feeds carefully written up on it so that he has a regular, planned diet. This can then be followed by anyone, so that if whoever looks after him unexpectedly cannot do so then his routine and diet

Feeding Our individual boards. Perkins (Friday Fayre) is by nature a thin horse, so he always has as much hay as he wants. At present he is unclipped and wears only a thick night rug (a Lavenham). With these instructions right outside his stable he should always have the right amount of hay and correct rugs.

will not have to be altered. Here, outside every horse's door we also have an individual board which states the horse's name and box number (also on the door), how much hay he has, dry or wet, what rugs he wears, what extra potions or creams he may be needing, and how much hay he should have left at late feed time last thing at night. There is then no reason or excuse for anything to be either forgotten or not known about, and the horse can be assured of the same regular care and feeding every day.

All the horses here who are stabled are fed three times a day: first thing in the morning, lunchtime and at teatime when all the work is finished. The horses who are actually competing, and any who are looking very poor and need building up, will also get a feed last thing at night, which should make their total feed easier to digest by evening out the time between four smaller meals. The first two feeds are smaller feeds than the last two, because the horses will be worked either during the morning or the afternoon and must not be given a large amount of food before exercise. The horses here are not worked at a similar time each day: the schedule is planned one day at a time as we see what has to be done and how many workers and riders we have. This is good for the young horse, as he learns early on to settle down and relax in his stable and then come out and work whenever he is wanted, rather than learning that a certain time of the day means it is time to start anticipating exercise. In the future he is, hopefully, going to become a seasoned competition horse, and may well have to do dressage one day at nine o'clock in the morning, and then perform at the next event late in the afternoon – if he is quite accustomed to irregular hours this should not bother him at all.

Adapting the Diet

As our horse's career progresses he will be working harder and will probably need more hard feed; when he becomes more mature and settled he may well require more again to keep him 'on his toes'. But there can never be hard and fast rules as to how much feed should be given. Every horse is different, and every season his feed and work patterns may alter. The old adage 'the eye of the master makes the horse fat' could not be more true: feeding is a constant process of observation and adaptation. A horse's work, his temperament and the ability of his rider all need to be taken into consideration.

Even hot or cold weather can change things. In cold weather the horse may be far more excitable, and when it is hot become positively lazy – and the seasons will also affect the feed value of grass and hay. The arrival of good spring grass and first class hay will often make a noticeable difference, and the hard feed may well need to be reduced to produce the same results as before. What we are going to feed must be planned ahead and ordered, particularly when nearing the haymaking season. Enough old hay to last right through the summer and autumn seasons is essential, as we do not want to be changing to new in mid-stream, so we have to work out how much will be needed and where it can be stored. It is no good waiting until the farmers have brought in their new hay and completely buried the old.

Presentation

To ensure the horse wants to eat his food he must always be presented with fresh, clean food. Every blade of hay left must be removed every morning, and not just 'topped up' so that old, musty-smelling hay is underneath the fresh. The temptation to pick up hay from the bed and put it back in the net or hayrack must also be resisted, as it will not be particularly appetising to the horse: it is vital to remember that we are trying to produce a top class athlete and he must be fed accordingly. Soaked hay must never be left until it becomes smelly – which it does very quickly – but should be fed as soon as the water has been drained.

Every feed bowl used to mix and carry the feeds must be scrubbed spotlessly clean after feeding each time – old bran and other cereals stuck onto the bowls will very quickly make the next meal smell and taste horrid. Every time after feeding is finished the feed scoops, spoons and bowls, and the bench where it is mixed, should look clean enough for human food. Before actually feeding each horse the manger should be wiped out so that it is clean – a handful of hay picked up as the feeder goes into each stable will do this quite adequately – but here I absolutely insist that every manger and water bowl or bucket is cleaned out impeccably once a day. This is done when mucking out in the morning: the horse is tied up in his stable (to a piece of string) and the first job is to clean the manger. Again, providing the job is done every single day then a handful of hay will clean it perfectly well in seconds, and it is only when the job has not been done regularly that it becomes a major and time-consuming chore of virtually chipping off rock-solid, congealed food remains.

In most of our stables we have automatic water bowls beside the mangers, and these are completely cleaned out daily at the same time. Old brackish water tastes (and smells) quite horrible, and a good supply of clean, fresh water is essential. Another reason for cleaning the manger and water before mucking out each horse is that the water bowl can then fill while the stable is being finished, and if it overfills or underfills it can be adjusted accordingly. We have found automatic waterers very good, especially after exercise as the horse cannot drink too much too quickly since the bowls do take a little while to fill – and, unlike a water bucket, they cannot be kicked over.

Bedding

Wood shavings are my preference for bedding for the event horse. We want a warm, comfortable bed that cannot be eaten if the horse is without hay, and shavings fit the bill. A good straw bed does look lovely if it is deep and made up of good straw, but one snag is that straw does hold the rather strong smell of horses (and then so do we), and personally it always makes me sneeze. This must be due to the dust factor and cannot be good for our horse's wind – the less dust around the better. Also it is jolly good to eat – a bit of a snag when we want our horse *not* to eat for a reason and then have to restrict him by tying him up or using a muzzle.

Paper makes good bedding, providing it is kept very clean and dry and mucked out well, but it does cost more than wood shavings. We have no supply of peat that I know of near here, and although it makes a good bed it can be dirty with a grey horse and tends to be a little dusty. Deep litter shaving beds are definitely my preference, ensuring that the horse cannot scrape his knees or hocks on the floor, and if it is mucked out well and kept topped up it makes a lovely bed, remarkably un-smelly and totally inedible.

Feeding During Competitions

When actually competing our feeding routine alters very little. I do not cut the hay or feed back the night before a one-day event but feed normally – trainers do not actually refuse to feed the human athlete the night before a game or race, and surely a hungry horse will be feeling as weak as we would if we had not eaten for hours?

In the morning he will have normal hard feed, but only a little hay – if he were going across country very early then the hay would be omitted. Certainly, no hay is fed in the lorry before an event (unless the horse was very late to start, when he might have a little while travelling); he would have no lunch before his start, and he would not be offered water within two hours of going across country. When he has finished, then he can have water, but only when he is not blowing and breathing heavily any more, and then only two or three inches at a time about every three or four minutes, until he has drunk his fill. The horse can then have a haynet or a bite of grass.

For his first feed after cross-country we will give him (several hours after finishing) a wet, easily digested, mostly bran feed, and then return to normal feeds after that. It is important never to be tempted to give the horse extra after an event as a reward for being so clever. The horse, just like us, will tend to have a smaller, not larger appetite than usual when he is tired, and if overfed will often completely go off the idea of eating at all. Over the years I have learnt that it is far better to feed smaller feeds than usual the night and morning after an event, which then get eaten right up and are eagerly anticipated, rather than overfeed or feed as normal and end up with a horse who will not eat for days.

When a horse does go on a hunger strike and refuse to eat at all I have found the best way of making him eat again is not to feed him any hard feed *at all* for several days, and then when he is really keen on the idea bring him back onto tiny feeds and build him back up to his old ration very slowly. A fit, healthy horse will manage perfectly well for several days on hay and grass alone, and when we have had to do this we have made a big effort almost to tease him as we feed the others, so that he feels jealous and left out and cannot wait to be fed again. Obviously it is important to work out *why* he is off his feed, so that it does not happen again. Was he offered a new feed, (a silly thing to do with a fit horse); was he fed with or in a dirty bowl (even more silly – a fit horse's appetite is more fragile and easily upset than that of an unfit horse); or was he simply being fed too much? Every horse has his own limit of feed, and invariably if we try to push him above it he will stop eating. Dazzle has shown me on two or three occasions that 12½lbs of hard feed is his limit – and 13lbs finishes his appetite. Occasionally a horse who has loved a certain feed will go off it completely – the skill of feeding is to realise this *before* he stops eating everything.

Before and during a three-day event my feed pattern again alters very little. The night before the cross-country normal hay is fed, but removed at ten o'clock. Normal late feed is then given as well as breakfast in the morning, providing the horse is due to start cross-country at least four hours later – if not, then a very small feed is given at least three and a half hours before kick off. With a late start he will be given a little hay, about 1lb, at breakfast time. His water will be left in all the time, but taken away two hours before the off. The horse must certainly not be dehydrated or totally starving or he will feel awful, but must feel empty enough to run for his life and produce his very best form.

The only other times that we will reduce the feeds is, firstly, on very long journeys, when every feed will be of the same composition as normal but half the amount, to ensure that with the forced inactivity of travelling there is no risk of colic. Great care must also be taken on long journeys to keep offering as much water as the horse wants. The second time we will cut the feed right back immediately to only 2-3lbs of easily digested wet bran is if for any reason the horse has to stop work. The hard feed must then stop also, or we will be asking for azoturia on return to work. Feeding the event horse is yet another learning process.

7 · PLANNED COMPETING

Very early in any young horse's competitive career we have to look ahead and think about competing at official events. To do this, the horse has to be registered with the relevant societies: the BSJA for show jumping, the BHS Horse Trial Group for eventing and the Dressage Group for dressage. Both owner and rider (if not one and the same) have to be members of each relevant discipline, and completing all these registrations takes time – and money.

Once the owner and rider have become Horse Trials Group members, the omnibus schedule for the next few months will arrive. This covers every event scheduled in the country with all their details, including how to go about entering and, as entries have to be posted several weeks before each event which has a ballot date, early planning and registration is essential in order to compete. No young horse can initially be registered nowadays without an up-to-date equine influenza vaccination certificate, and if this programme has not been started well in advance there will be no BHS eventing ahead. Show jumping registration is much easier, as although horses, owners and riders have to be members of the BSJA, most novice shows, particularly indoor ones, take entries on the day, so there is not quite the necessity to register months ahead.

A Planned Progression

Even at my horse's very earliest unaffiliated shows I try to have a long-term plan mapped out in the back of my mind, all the way to International level. His competition career should be a steady learning process as he goes up the ladder, and the timing of his progression through each grade is very important. His first Pre-Novice or Novice event should be at the start or at least in the first half of the eventing year, so that we can do a number of events in his first season and finish with him well established and happily coping as a Novice event horse. Usually when young horses have a break they seem to come back to competition slightly greener than they were at the end of the season before, and for that reason it is preferable not to go up a grade just before a break. One of the joys of the older horse is that they do not forget anything when they have a holiday. Still, the young horse is usually back to his old form within two or three competitions, if taken carefully.

Once we are out and about doing official events, and I know that the horse is capable of and ready to upgrade to Intermediate, then this is an

---

(p161) Master Fiddler jumping a big spread drop fence at Gatcombe confidently, economically and at speed. He looks comfortable and easy, which is reflected in my own position – no exaggerated sitbacks from either of us!

important step to plan for and to time correctly. To upgrade to Intermediate a horse has to have won over twenty points. The first six prize winners in every section of every novice event win points (if there are an insufficient number of starters the points for lower places may not be awarded, but on the rare occasion that this happens it usually only affects the fifth and sixth places at most). The winner gains six points, the second five points and so on, down to one point for sixth place.

Winning points can sometimes seem impossible; we have all had horses who seem always to finish seventh, and occasionally the opposite occurs – a horse who is incapable of *not* clocking up the points. Chatsby and Halloween Time were both like that for me: they would do an outstandingly good dressage nearly always, followed by a clear show jumping and start the cross-country with a lead of several points. I then had to be very careful to make sure that we did not go too fast and win too much too soon. It is not necessary to upgrade before you are ready; time faults are gained cross-country for exceeding the optimum time, and as this is usually a fast time which it is not easy to be 'inside', all that has to be done with the true novice to ensure not too good a result is to canter round. As one time fault is awarded for every three seconds over the time, a slow round will only pick up a low prize at best. So upgrading should happen to the aware, intelligent rider only when he or she considers the horse is ready.

Picking Up Speed

Although a good dressage and clear show jumping are needed for good results, exactly when a horse is upgraded depends largely on when he is taken fast across country. Going fast and producing a good result is not just a question of galloping flat out. This may work once or twice, but it will not pay dividends in the long term. As with all his training, the horse must move on into gallop still completely under control, listening to the rider, and still in balance.

The way the course is ridden and walked is also of great importance. We now want to go the quickest route available that we can jump safely, covering the least amount of ground possible and wasting the minimum of time. Still, however much I may want to win – and this applies at any level for me – I do not want to jump a fence that I am not totally happy about both for myself and for my horse. Every rider must learn what type of fence they ride well, and what type they do not – and then with every single horse learn the same about them. All the top riders will jump one route through an alternative with one horse, and then may take another way with a second horse – the skill lies in finding out which way works best for each combination of horse and rider. Only the rider can know that answer, and he must be confident enough to follow his intuition.

If I am asked for advice on alternative fences I may well advise one definite route, but may equally well say that I am happy with two or three routes, and really which one to choose has to be the rider's own decision. But whichever way is chosen it must be decided beforehand and *stuck to* – too many errors at this type of fence come from riders who have still not decided which way to go as they approach the fence. The time advantage of the 'quick way' also has to be weighed against the risk involved: for the gain of two or three seconds there is not a lot of point in risking anything, but if more time is at stake then maybe this will outweigh the risk. One thing I have learnt, and that is that hindsight will always show us the way we should have gone. When trying to do well it is also important to concentrate all the time when course walking, and to look ahead and assess the fastest route to the next fence. A quick getaway from each jump is needed, and it is easy to forget that two seconds wasted at each jump can add up to at least forty overall, which means fourteen time faults – more than a few.

Upgrading

Once we have decided that the horse is ready to go on and upgrade, it still needs careful planning both ahead of time and at each event. It is a great help when events are efficient and have a well run scoring system; the score for each horse's dressage can easily be on the scoreboard by the time he has show jumped, and I always try to assess roughly where he will be placed in his section by the start of the cross-country, and then decide whether or not we have a chance and whether I should be hurrying this time or not.

After the close of entries, clearly stated on each event's schedule, a horse may still compete if he has subsequently upgraded. So if it can be planned that he upgrades with two or three more events still to run in, it can be an added bonus. I like to upgrade and then go straight on and do several Intermediate events, while my horse is still confident and going well from his Novice events, and then stop until next season. When planning for the following season with a fairly newly upgraded horse I like to start if possible with an Open Novice class, which is a relatively new class with Intermediate dressage and show jumping, but Novice cross-country. This is ideal for my young horse to regain his confidence and re-establish how easy it is, and how much he likes cross-country. Then on we go to a season of Intermediate events, and I have to think about when we are going to do our first three-day event.

The First Three-Day Event

Novice three-day events are a marvellous introduction to the very different sport of the three-day event. I do not necessarily always do a Novice three-day event with a horse – if it fits in to the schedule both of my own year as a rider and into the horse's calendar, then fine, but if not I will wait until he is more experienced from his one-day events and go straight to an Intermediate three-day event or even a one star CCI, the lowest level of International event which is built to Intermediate dimensions. For the inexperienced rider, though, the Novice three-day (and even two-day) event is a tremendous thing to do. Intermediate horses are eligible as well as Novice, and to tackle all the new things of a three-day event without too demanding a course cross-country can only be a good thing. Apart from the additional work needed beforehand in preparation, there are many different aspects at a three-day event (including new rules to learn), and the Novice class is a great place to tackle the job for the first time.

The first three-day event for the horse should come at the end of a successful season. When he is competing at Intermediate level he is still learning all the time, and with this in mind he should be run in about six one-day events before the three-day. If we are in the spring season the first event would probably be in March, and we must then map out a regular schedule of events building up to the three-day event, probably in late May. Then afterwards a break, *definitely*.

Taking a Break

When a horse has been produced to a peak of fitness and to the maximum of his ability, his muscles are indisputably going to be very tired. Yet often after a three-day event the horse will seem almost fresh: this is not a true freshness, but more a kind of over-exhausted prolonged 'high' which is the result of all the adrenalin pumping at the big event. It compares rather well to a small child who, after a long-awaited and anticipated party comes home to bed and is so over-tired and excited that sleep is impossible. The horse *must* be given a break, and allowed to wind down and relax both physically and mentally. Horses who have been run again quickly after a three-day event have more often than not disappointed their connections with a mediocre performance – and I have known several who have strained themselves in doing so. They do need and deserve a break after their exertions, and ours go straight out in the field for a few hours the first day we are home. When they are still tired from travelling they seem to settle very quickly and graze in the field – maybe the opportunity to eat lovely grass again is irresistible.

Even if the holiday is only to be for a few weeks, particularly with a late spring three-day event, our horses still build up with a few more hours grazing each day until they are out all day. They come in at night so we can check them thoroughly, and they have two feeds, one evening and one morning, to keep condition on them, and after at least three weeks hols it is back to work and the build up to our next event. With a short break like this it will only take about six weeks for the horse to be fit enough for the first one-day event of the next season. If my horse has gone well to date, then this time around we will build up through approximately six more one-days to another, slightly more demanding three-day event, possibly even going abroad. Then it is time to rough him off again and let him have a good long winter break, and next time he comes back to work it will be for his third year as an event horse – this time hopefully as a young Advanced event horse.

Sponsorship

Once our young event horse starts to compete seriously, how can his whole career be financed? To have a farm or some land at home is a tremendous advantage, but even with hay, straw and some feed coming from the farm there are still many items which have to be paid for. All the roadwork means a lot of shoes, and shoeing bills are never small. Merry Sovereign used to wear an ordinary set of shoes out in one week, unbelievable as that may sound, and even with expensive steel welded into them they would only last two or three weeks – I dread to think how much money I spent over the years on his shoes. Horses seem to have an uncanny ability to chew and break down their stables, rip and damage their rugs and, worse, to injure themselves, and carpentry, saddlery and veterinary work are all pricey. Affiliation and registration fees all cost money, as do the entries, while the diesel and petrol bill for travelling to events – and when horse hunting in the first place – can be a nasty shock. Finally our own clothes, both to survive and work in at home and to look smart in competition, are an expensive little item, so the event horse does produce a financial headache even before we count the stable rent or rates, and light and water. I do not enjoy listing the many items that we all have to pay for: it produces some sobering thoughts.

When my sister Sally initially started to compete seriously after she had left school, it was essential that her horses were a business and, hopefully, paid their costs. Not wanting to sell all the horses she produced, she started to take other people's horses at livery, either to break or to bring on, and also to teach people here at home on their own horses or ponies. My parents encouraged her to take her BHSAI so that she was a qualified instructor, and when I left school four years later I took my pony club A test and BHSAI and joined Sally (who by now was a highly qualified BHSI), determined that we would manage to build up a small business to finance our own competing – for some extraordinary reason I had a burning ambition to 'get to the top'. Slowly, as satisfied owners took their horses home going better for hunting or competing, the standard of horses sent to us improved, though we still had, and have today, all sorts and shapes and sizes, and enjoy working with them all.

When Sally married and left home, we then had a few horses here that I was competing on for their owners, and the whole business of riding for someone else was another aspect about which I had to learn. My own two horses were competing, but the odd ride came my way as well which was marvellous experience, as well as being the only way then that I could possibly have had several horses to compete on, as neither my parents nor I could have afforded to buy any more. Remembering to telephone the horse's owners regularly with progress reports; being ready and willing to show him off if they wanted to pop in and see their horse work; looking after them at competitions or, if they could not come, ringing them that night to report how it all went – was marvellous training and practice for my sponsorship today. No owner, whether private or commercial, can be expected to own horses for the sake of it – they want to be involved (at both good and bad times, we hope) and enjoy their horses and the sport. The best practice for any young rider wanting sponsorship is to go out there and find horses to ride for other people, and learn all about owners.

What the Sponsor has to Offer

First of all, what exactly does a sponsor provide and involve for a rider? Most of us who are lucky enough to have sponsors are paid a lump sum, which in effect works like a leasing fee, and the horses can then, after official approval from the British Equestrian Federation, compete in the sponsor's name. This lump sum helps to pay the bills and expenses and, providing it remains less than the total cost involved in producing the horses (not difficult!), it does not jeopardise the rider's amateur status. How this money is spent is then up to the rider in most cases. It is an enormous help, for which we are most grateful but of course it does not pay every bill, so I still take horses at livery here and, together with the girls who work for me, do quite a lot of breaking in. My head girl and I help the local pony clubs and riding clubs who come here for jumping and cross-country sessions, and generally try to bring in the extra cash needed to finance the horses, and of course the odd horse has to be sold on to help keep the sums right. Most riders have a similar lifestyle of

Sponsorship Sweep the Board and myself in our sponsor, Gateway Foodmarkets Ltd's, livery. The jacket and all the horse's rugs have the company logo, and with several people and horses dressed like this as a team, and with the horsebox sprayed to match, it gives the horses' owners a great boost.

struggling along to keep going, and to have some sort of sponsorship is a great relief.

What the Rider has to Offer

In return for the financial help, we as riders can offer a certain amount of publicity. The horses can wear clothing with the company or private owner's logo, as can the rider and helpers involved, providing no logo is worn when actually competing in the ring. Commentators, both live at events and on television programmes, can, and frequently do, name and talk about the owners and, of course, they can come along to the competitions and watch their horse and rider, hopefully, do well. How much value any sponsor gets from their involvement is largely up to the rider, who has to realise that he cannot just take the money and run – it has to be worked for. But having extra supporters around can be great fun, and we have certainly had some excellent times with Mr and Mrs Francis who are from Gateways Food Markets Ltd, my sponsors – even when they came with me to a three-day event at Breda in Holland to watch Master Control, and I fell at the first fence!

Finding a Sponsor

Finding a sponsor is not easy. There are a lot of extremely talented sportsmen and women who would jump at the opportunity of sponsorship in all sports, not just in our own, and to interest a company in the first place you really need a toe in the door – an introduction from someone who knows someone. Then it is a question of selling the idea to them, and if the person involved can become really interested in the whole concept then you are away – but it takes a lot of hard work to get this far. My advice to someone trying to find some sort of sponsorship for the first time is not to set your sights (and figures) too high. A little help at first can grow with careful management, enjoyment and, with luck, good results, to larger things – and the young event horse may find himself looking like a very smart chap in his special livery as he competes for a new 'owner'.

8 · THE YOUNG EVENT HORSE

The young event horse is now ready for his final step – into Advanced one- and three-day events. Building up to a major Advanced International event, I will only compete in three or four one-day events in preparation. By now the horse should know his job, and should simply do enough events to put an edge on his fitness, remind him of the problems (and joys) of cross-country, settle his performance and then go on to the three-day event with a real 'edge', feeling fresh and ready to go.

The Build Up

With the spring season our horse will be coming back to work after a long lay-off. The end of the event season is in October, and in preparation for either Bramham or Badminton, our spring national Advanced events, we bring the horse into work at the beginning of January. If the horse has had a soundness problem at the end of the previous season then we will follow our vet's orders implicitly – usually weeks of very boring, quite essential walking exercise. If there have been no earlier hiccups then we start to hack normally, with short trots and even hand canters, from day one. Horses in the field – at least here anyway – do not only walk, they often trot and canter, and even charge about like lunatics, and if they are fit enough to do that by themselves then they can certainly cope with a little trot work. By doing this, we have certainly had far less trouble with over-fresh horses wanting to buck and behave badly when riding out, which has to be a lot safer for everyone on the roads.

The first few days we will do about forty minutes' hacking, and be building up to an hour by the end of the first week. Two more weeks and we will have gradually increased to about an hour and a half's work and then after three weeks it is time to start schooling on the flat. Then on to a little jumping, and we can begin to think of a few small competitions.

Schooling

How frequently one should school is really an unanswerable question. Primarily, it must depend on how much each horse needs and this will vary with every single individual, as will the time needed for riding in at competitions. Some horses will settle with only half an hour's work – Delphy Kingfisher always did. Some will like to come out several times

(pp170-1) Delphy Kingfisher winning the advanced class at Molland in 1981, the year he won the Calcutta Cup for the leading horse nationally. He was a horse who needed the minumum of schooling at home and would perform as well as ever with very little preparation — the opposite to his relatives Merry Sovereign and Delphy Dazzle.

and merely wander about looking at everything, and settle in their own time before being seriously ridden in – Friday Fayre does. And some will need to hack seriously or lunge and do a lot of work before they will concentrate – Merry Sovereign and Delphy Dazzle are both of this type.

The same principle will apply to working at home. If a horse works well and improves all the time with schooling once or twice a week then that is probably all he needs, but a horse who is learning a new lesson or who cannot settle may have to school every day. Perhaps one horse will work at his best after half an hour of training, but another will need far longer to reach his best – experimenting is the only way to find the best method for each horse, and even then constant adjustment is needed as the horse matures, changes and grows up.

Jumping schooling is very much the same. I like to do enough to keep my horses settled and rideable, but work mainly over trotting poles and the same two basic grids over which they very first learnt to jump. Although jumping has to be fun for the horse, he must still accept the same basic principles of being ridden as with all his work throughout his career, and working correctly over trotting poles and grid work is the best way to ensure that discipline and to keep his style and method over the fence as correct as possible – with all the galloping over fences across country it is only too easy to develop a flat, fast jump which will have poles down in the show jumping, so we have to keep reminding our horse how to jump round and high again.

Cantering quietly over fences in a schooled canter with an even rhythm is also valuable occasionally, but in the build up to the spring season we go to indoor shows virtually every weekend and so (providing they are jumping well) may only do some grid work between shows if I feel they need to settle or jump better in the air. As a matter of course I do not school over the cross-country fences here once my horses have started their BHS career. If a problem arose then obviously I would, but I feel that if they are going well then the jump will become correct with show jumping training, their gallop will also improve as we do the canter work, and the best training of all for cross-country is to meet new problems in competition armed with confidence gained from the work at home.

The Fitness Programme

Every time the fitness programme for a three-day event will vary. This is not only because each horse is different, but also because as the one-day event dates beforehand change so must the preparation. With our marvellous hills and roadwork here we do not use the interval training method, but do canter work in one continuous block each time. There are

Final Programme for Advanced Three-Day Event

	Monday	Tuesday	Wednesday	Thursday	Friday	Saturday	Sunday
Week 6 2hrs roadwork daily	Canter 12 min			Canter 8 min			Open Intermediate One-Day Event: 2 miles
Week 7 Roadwork as Week 6	Day off: 20 min walk	Walking exercise (see p175)	Back to normal roadwork		Canter 12 min		
Week 8 Roadwork as Week 6	Canter 13 min			Canter 10 min			Advanced One-Day Event: 2½ miles
Week 9 Roadwork as Week 6	Day off: 20 min walk	Walking exercise (see p175)	Back to normal roadwork		Canter 13 min		
Week 10 2½hrs roadwork on non-canter days, 2hrs on canter days	Canter 15 min			Canter 4min then twice up 4 furlong gallop fast			Canter 16 min
Week 11 2hrs roadwork daily			Canter 14 min			Advanced One-Day Event: 2½ miles	Day off: 20 min walk
Week 12 2½hrs roadwork on non-canter days, 2hrs on canter days	Walking exercise (see p175)	Back to normal roadwork		Canter 15 min			Canter 17 min
Week 13 2½hrs roadwork Mon and Tues, then 2hrs daily			Canter 4 min, then twice up 4 furlong gallop fast			Canter 18 min	
Week 14 1½hrs roadwork daily		Canter 10 min		Advanced Three-Day Event	Advanced Three-Day Event	Advanced Three-Day Event: Cross-country 4 miles	Advanced Three-Day Event

certainly many systems that will produce a fit athlete, whether equine or human, but whichever system is used it must be religiously adhered to, and again I map out a programme on a calendar.

My initial system for getting a young horse fit for the top level would vary very little from horse to horse the first time, but I will be observing and feeling how well it is working in order to adapt it next time around to suit each individual horse. By six weeks before the first one-day event, usually an Open Intermediate class to have an easy run, we will have built up to two hours' roadwork every day. As with the early Novice horse, the roadwork is kept up every day, and the canter every three days (occasionally four), building up to twelve minutes a week before the event. If the second event was two weeks later, probably an Advanced event, then the canter work would carry on increasing after one shorter canter the first time. Unlike with a series of one-day events, the fitness has to build up now to a higher level for later, so that the canter work must be a progression towards the three-day event that incorporates the one-day but still allows the horse to feel fresh and run well at them, and recover easily afterwards.

With another advanced event three weeks later the canter work will now build up to about sixteen to eighteen minutes, at the same three to four day intervals. If I felt that the horse would benefit from a little more work I might increase the roadwork occasionally, and if we go out for about two and a quarter hours from here we can get in three good big hills which we trot up. We can also use a lovely forty-acre field which has marvellous slopes to trot and occasionally canter *slowly* up. It is important to remember again, though, not to stress the horses too often – they do need three days to recover, and excess hill work *every* day will produce back leg strains and not fit horses. Only experience can tell a rider how much to do: the golden rule is that you cannot make a horse fitter than fit, and true fitness will come with a steady, consistent build up, not with excess work.

Depending again on the individual horse I may do fast work at home, but if we have gone fast at the events then often this is enough. With a long break after the last one-day event before the three-day, then maybe the work should increase again and fast work at roughly ten-day intervals can be necessary. Then I do almost interval train: I will canter for three minutes to settle my horse; then go fast (again with a 'gear' in hand) along our four furlong (half-mile) track with the uphill incline to finish; then walk back down the slope, which takes about two minutes; go gradually back into canter for two furlongs, returning to the start of our meadow, and then fast back along and up again. For a final workout this may be done three times, but usually only twice, and it certainly makes the horse blow

2

Hill work Starting up the hill in trot (1) the horse looks a little hollow and is not really working, but by the top (2) he has dropped his head and is really using all his body.

1

Fast work (below) This is an ideal incline on which to do fast work as it is not *too* steep, yet really makes the horses work.

and work, and puts an edge on his fitness.

For the final week before the three-day event the roadwork is reduced to about an hour and a half, and we do shorter canters. Enough work is needed to settle the horse, but he should arrive at the big event feeling 100 per cent fit, fresh and with 'an edge', and ready to go. Getting this right is all a question of timing, and training horses is a constant learning process which, when it really comes right, is extremely satisfying.

Mental Fitness

Keeping the horse's frame of mind right while working at home is often more difficult with the experienced horses than with the very young ones. For the first few seasons of work every ride and every canter is an adventure, and it is no problem to keep the horse's interest. An enthusiastic, keen horse will be no problem to get fit whereas the bored, disinterested horse is – he will only slop along whether hacking out, schooling or cantering, and the more he is ridden out to make him work the more fed up and sour he will tend to become.

Throughout the training process a very careful eye must be kept on every horse's attitude, and he must be worked with suitable company to keep up his enthusiasm. This does not necessarily mean always riding him with another horse: I have known several horses who have loved working alone and seemed literally to loathe other horses. Master Control, although easy to ride at an event with others around, was like this, and was always a joy to hack out alone and never so happy with company. Master Fiddler, a very easy horse for anyone to ride out on, will go along very quietly and nicely behind on the roads, yet gradually start looking bored and more and more sulky. Then when he is later being schooled he can be in such a bad mood that he is not co-operative at all, and so now he goes out either in front of or only with one other. We do generally try to ride out in pairs so that every horse is basically working in front, which not only keeps their interest but also ensures (particularly with the young horses) that they are always being brave and going past new things without taking a lead – cross-country training again.

Canter work is very much the same. Some horses will very quickly realise it is hard work and a pointless exercise and become bored; others to begin with will not really get the message and will not go forward properly – these will need to canter in company. Yet others, Delphy Dazzle for example, will always want to go faster and will be far too silly if worked in company. If a horse does need to be cantered with another to teach him to want to go on and enjoy himself, then we use one of the older, settled horses (Fiddler has been good at this job for us).

Two experienced riders are a great help when first cantering a young horse 'upsides' another. The older horse must be kept straight and in an even pace while the youngster is encouraged to go beside him but slightly behind – about a neck. This will hopefully encourage him to pull and try to keep up and eventually overtake his friend, which is what we want. To keep the interest, we can drop the young horse back so that he feels he is being left behind, and then 'allow' him to accelerate and catch up, thinking it is his own idea to pull on. Playing with the pace and the two horses' relative positions will make a big difference to the way they are working, and can do wonders for the uninterested horse. If an older horse is *really* bored then a new place to work can often transform him, and it can be well worthwhile hacking or travelling to other gallops to keep him interested.

Adapting the Programme

The programme I have mapped out has evolved from working at home here in Devon, where we do have wonderful hills and yet also good level fields for canter work. Different situations and land will inevitably dictate different methods – having no hills, for example, would be a nasty shock to me if we ever moved.

Mark Todd lives on the edge of Salisbury Plain, and so has virtually no roadwork but limitless grass and tracks. Before the World Championships in Gawler, South Australia, in 1986 my horses were all based at his yard while Dazzle and the rest of the team horses were in quarantine with the riders at nearby Wylye. Every day I travelled to Mark's yard and worked my horse in his country. My system did then have to alter a little: we tended to do more trotting up gradual slopes, and our cantering work would just follow natural tracks and gradients. Ian Stark also had his horses there, but his usual ground in Scotland is old heath and moorland so there was not a lot of difference for him.

Monitoring Fitness

One way of monitoring and assessing a horse's fitness is to keep a record of his pulse and respiration rates after work, and how quickly they recover, and I always feel slightly guilty when I say I do not do this. In rather an old fashioned way, perhaps, I believe that the trainer's eye and rider's feel are the best judges – but time and experience is the only way to develop the knowledge to be able to assess fitness, and pulse and respiration monitoring is advised by most American eventing trainers. Ever since I was a small child I have had the importance of a fit horse – or pony, in my early hunting days – drummed into me, and the advice I would give to a novice rider is let an older, more experienced person watch their horse work occasionally and say what they think, and then learn from this and from how the horse feels at the end of each competition. You could, of course, study the American system and do it all on paper – but still, the old British methods have worked for many years, and they do allow for the differences between individual horses. The truly fittest horse is the one who finishes his competition in the best shape.

Other Training Methods

Nowadays different methods of training horses are becoming fashionable. Equine swimming pools are used by some racing trainers and have been by event riders. If a horse has a problem that means he cannot be ridden – for example, a sore back or even foot – but has no actual leg strain, then swimming could be useful to keep up his fitness while he cannot canter with a rider, but I do not like the idea of swimming a horse who has had a strain and then returning him straight back into the programme when all appears well. A strain must recover best with rest, and then careful slow work before a build up back to the old work level. Just looking good and trotting up sound does not mean that a horse is necessarily fit enough to work hard, and the muscles that are going to be needed must have been worked regularly and be in good shape. Our vet once said he loved swimming for getting horses fit – if they were going in for swimming races! Basically, to get your horse fit by doing similar work to the job in question has to be the best answer, although substituting the odd swim for a canter would obviously be fine and can even be great fun for the horse.

Horse walkers, a kind of mechanical lunge circle for any number of horses, have been used by many people, but must be far more boring and of less educational value than the variety of hacking through different country. Of course, if there is not enough time to ride properly horse walkers must be a better alternative than standing in the stable.

Another machine I have seen used in racing stables is a treadmill. Here the horse goes into a stall of a similar size to a partition in a lorry or trailer, usually with a slightly uphill-sloped floor. The floor slowly moves backwards so that the horse has to walk forwards to stay still – it sounds most odd, but horses do seem to settle in it and work rather as they would on roadwork. Rather as with horse walkers, the treadmill is probably better than no exercise at all but is still not as good as riding out, and I feel it must ultimately be character-destroying for the event horse.

Bitting

As each horse develops through his career one thing that often changes, even very early on in his Novice events, is what bit he will go best in. Here the young horses usually start their work in jointed rubber snaffles, and if this feels good and they are happy then this is the bit they stay in. Generally, though, my horses have felt a little too strong in this as they start to compete, and we have moved on to a metal bit. Personally, I prefer the feel of riding most horses in a thinner rather than a very thick mouthpiece: it feels lighter, and I do not like or find it easy to ride a horse who is very heavy in my hands. Really, when a horse starts to feel as if another bit would suit better it is a question of trial and error, and here we have a great collection of bits to try.

Merry Sovereign was my first International horse who was completely home-produced from scratch, and he always went in dressage, show jumping and cross-country both at home and in competition in a loose ring German snaffle and dropped noseband (with the addition of a loose running martingale for show jumping in competition). As trainer and jockey, I thought I was very clever. Then along came Delphy Kingfisher, who went quite beautifully in every phase in a jointed rubber snaffle and cavesson. My ego became enormous – and then when he upgraded to Intermediate he started to pull. For nearly a year the key to the brakes was impossible to find, until in desperation I tried a gag snaffle – never imagining it would work, as he always pulled with a high head carriage which a gag often produces itself – and it was magic.

This experience taught me that there are not many rules to individual bitting. Taking a strong hold when the adrenalin starts pumping often seems to be as much of a mental problem as a schooling problem, and to me whatever bit, noseband or martingale works (provided it is allowed by the rules) has to be the one to use. But once the brakes are discovered, then they should only be used *in competition* unless absolutely necessary – the horse who has learnt to pull will quickly find a way around another new bit given half a chance, but often if he learns to respect and be comfortable in his jumping or cross-country bit he will accept it each time and never be a real problem again. The more experienced horse will tend to realise that cross-country is yet another job to settle to whereas at first, if he is of a temperament that loves the whole thing, the excitement of being allowed to gallop to places unknown can definitely go to his head.

Holidays Delphy Dazzle and Master Fiddler on their winter holidays. Both come in at night, and give the distinct impression that they cannot wait to get back into work and on the road again.

Finally, then, our young event horse is the finished article – a three-day event horse who knows his job. After all the years of preparation and hard work he should stay there for many years, and if he is looked after properly he will. Generally speaking, two three-day events each year are plenty; very occasionally I have ridden a horse in three in a year, but then have done only very few one-days. Three one-day events and one three-day event per season – spring and autumn – is good guideline: it is very tempting to be greedy and want more from a super horse, but surely it is more fun if he lasts for ten years (and some have) at this level rather than burns out in two or three? As accurately as possible, using my not-quite-good-enough memory and my records, the inmates of our establishment today are listed below with their careers with me as a guide. The intention was to have similar programmes for each, but with the inevitable hiccups of life they have varied.

Merry Sovereign

Bay, 16.2hh. Born 1968. Bought by me as a 'just backed' five-year-old in late summer, competed in hunter trials and indoor show jumping that winter, took part in his first novice BHS event in March as a six-year-old.

First year eventing 1974: won two novice events in the spring season, upgraded to Intermediate early autumn, competed at Intermediate and then Wylye three-day event.

Second year: competed Intermediate, the finished second at Punchestown (Ireland) CCI in spring. Competed Advanced level and placed Burghley CCI in autumn.

Third year: competed in one Open Intermediate, one Advanced, placed Badminton CCI. Short-listed for Olympic games in autumn season and injured himself in the final trial, subsequently rested for remainder of the autumn season – his only season in a ten-year career without competing in a three-day event.

Fourth year: again two one-day events pre-Badminton, then two more pre-Burghley European Championships, where he was in the winning team.

Subsequent years until 1983: Sovereign competed in no more than four or five one-day events each year and another twelve major three-day events at home and abroad, including one more European Championship and the 1982 World Championships, where he was to finish sixth individual – our best result. He completed six consecutive Badmintons and in 1984, as a fifteen-year-old in his tenth year of three-day eventing, finished fifth in Breda (Holland) and fourth in Felstebo (Sweden). I felt the time had come to retire him from competition then, and he had several seasons happily hunting. His job in life now is to accompany the others in the field when they are on holiday – he is still ridden occasionally and feels as young as ever.

DELPHY DAZZLE

Bay, 16.3hh. Born 1976. Bought by me as an unbroken three-year-old in the late autumn. Backed and ridden on that winter, and taken to a few spring baby shows with a view to competing in several and then turning him away. He was *so* naughty and over-exuberant outside the ring that his holiday never happened, and we progressed on through his four-year-old summer to BSJA jumping and, eventually, manageable behaviour in public. He competed in hunter trials that autumn, and a few indoor shows that winter.

First year eventing 1981: as a five-year-old, won one event in the spring season and upgraded to Intermediate in the middle of the autumn season, competing in one Intermediate event to finish his first year (not by intention, a difficult course which he coped with brilliantly).

Second year: competed in Intermediate one-day events and Breda (Holland) CCI in the spring. More Intermediates followed in the autumn, with Wylye CCI at the end of the season.

Third year: several open Intermediates to start with in the spring, then one Advanced one-day, followed by Rome (Italy) CCI which was very much Advanced standard. In the autumn season Burghley was planned, but after competing in one Advanced class and Gatcombe Open International One-Day Championships I was injured in a bad fall at Taunton horse trials and Dazzle had to wait, as he was sidelined for the rest of the season with my other horses.

Fourth year: rider still out of action until the autumn, so after a year off through no fault of his own the previous year's plan came into action – two Advanced one-day events and Burghley CCI. Thanks to Dazzle's career having started so early, the year without competing hardly mattered and he was at his first Burghley still at the age of only eight.

Fifth year: two one-days then Badminton, then in the autumn three one-days and Burghley European Championships.

Since then Dazzle has started and completed two major three-day events every year, including taking me to Australia and a World Championship team gold medal. Badminton is our current aim again, and hopefully as long a career as Merry Sovereign's will give us a few more years of fun.

MASTER FIDDLER

Liver chestnut, 16.2hh. Born 1979. Bought by me as a five-year-old in November, he had already completed two hunter trials. We indoor show jumped that winter and started eventing the following spring.

First year eventing: Placed all the way through the spring season, he won once, upgraded in the autumn and was then placed in one Intermediate.

Second year: After several Intermediate events Fiddler was placed fourth in the Madrid three-day event, and then in the autumn went to both Rotherfield and Chatsworth three-day events, but did only two other one-day events.

Third year: After one Open Intermediate, competed in Advanced one-day events, then Le Touquet CCI, and in the autumn went to Gatcombe Open Championships and Boekelo CCI.

Fourth year: Badminton, after two one-day events: then we missed starting Burghley through a fall of mine on another horse, and went to Boekelo again.

Fifth year: Badminton again, I hope.

FRIDAY FAYRE

Chestnut, 17hh. Born 1980. Bought by me as a five-year-old in early autumn when he had just started competing at unaffiliated baby level. Competed subsequently in a few hunter trials, and show jumped indoors through that winter, starting BHS events the following spring.

First year eventing 1986: although often well placed, with a sometimes weak dressage he was still just Novice grade at the end of the year.

Second year: upgraded in the spring season and competed in several late spring/summer Intermediates, competed and was placed at Hasselt (Belgium) CCI in August. With only a short season left, competed in two more Intermediates and then an Open two-day event in Holland.

Third year: competed in Intermediate, then in two Advanced one-day events. Entered for Bramham CCI but hit himself the week before so was withdrawn. In the autumn season he competed well in three Intermediate events and two Advanced, and did a fairly pleasing dressage at Chatsworth CCI – which was rained into cancellation before the cross-country.

Turned out for his holiday after a not ideal year, last winter (1988) Friday Fayre was found one afternoon to be very lame. He was scanned and discovered to have a broken pedal bone in his near forefoot. Mr Attenburrow, our marvellous vet, is very optimistic that he will make a total recovery and return to top level eventing in time – but certainly 1988 was *not* his year.

Halloween Time

Dark brown, 17hh. Born 1982. Bought by me as a 'just backed' four-year-old in September. Competed in two hunter trials and then indoor show jumped during the winter.

First year eventing 1987: as a five-year-old, he really did almost too well and, frequently starting cross-country with a very good score, upgraded in the early part of the autumn season. Jumped beautifully around three Intermediates and then an Open two-day event in Holland.

Second year: we tried to go slower. Started Intermediate again late spring, and carried on after three one-day events to Holker Hall Novice three-day event in June. Had a short break, then did five more Intermediates and Waregem (Belgium) CCI in September.

Third year: still to come, but will hopefully consist of several Intermediates followed by two Advanced one-days and then either Windsor or Bramham three-day event. His autumn target will, with luck, be Chatsworth CCI or a similar Advanced standard three-day abroad. Then fourth year Burghley, I hope, with Badminton to follow the year after, when he will be a nine-year-old.

(pp188-9) Friday Fayre at the beginning of his career, and looking quite confident at being asked to hurry for one of the first times. There is a big ditch in front of this fence and he is showing exactly how the young horse should look up and over holes in the ground – and how much he enjoys his job.

SWEEP THE BOARD

Dark brown, 16.3hh. Born 1983. Bought by me last autumn as a five-year-old and currently show jumping indoors. He had competed at unaffiliated events with his previous owners, and should be making his BHS 'debut' in the spring.

TREWAN

Bay, 16.2hh. Born 1981. Bought by me as a six-year-old in the early winter. He had competed and won several open hunter trials, and show jumped up to Foxhunter and Grade C classes (larger than novice BHS events). We jumped through that winter indoors, and went to the first event of the spring season.

First year: as an already fairly experienced seven-year-old, after competing in and being placed at several Novice events we went to Chepstow Intermediate to qualify for Holker Novice three-day. At Holker he went extremely well and was second; a few more Novice one-day events followed, he upgraded and was then placed in several Intermediates.

Second year: to come, but hopefully one Intermediate followed by Windsor Intermediate three-day, with a build up to an Advanced three-day in the autumn.

At the moment I am again searching for one or two more prospects for the future. Sweep the Board will, all being well, be ready for the coming season, but another youngster to bring on as well will, hopefully, arrive soon. As always, it is back to the start of the old cycle and, like everyone else, my heart still leaps when I hear of a super-sounding horse to go and see – maybe a star is waiting there and we will be off again.

ACKNOWLEDGEMENTS

With thanks to Lucinda Green for persuading me to start writing, and to my parents and sister Sally for all their help, backing and encouragement throughout my eventing career. And, of course, to my marvellous horses – Merry Sovereign and Delphy Dazzle especially – who have given me so much fun and pleasure.

INDEX

Figures in *italics* denote illustrations

DAVID & CHARLES EQUESTRIAN TITLES

BEHAVIOUR PROBLEMS IN HORSES *Susan McBane*
BREEDING AND TRAINING A HORSE OR PONY *Ann Sutcliffe*
CHAMPION HORSES AND PONIES *Pamela Macgregor-Morris*
COMPLEAT HORSE *Johannes E. Flade*
DRESSAGE Begin the Right Way *Lockie Richards*
EQUINE FITNESS *Dr David Snow and Colin Vogel*
GOING THE DISTANCE A Manual of Long-distance Riding *Sue Parslow*
GYMKHANA! *Lesley Eccles and Linda Burgess*
THE HEAVY HORSE MANUAL *Nick Rayner and Keith Chivers*
THE HORSE AND THE LAW *Donald Cassell*
HORSE BREEDING *Peter Rossdale*
HORSE DRIVING TRIALS The Art of Competitive Coachmanship *Tom Coombs*
THE HORSE'S HEALTH FROM A TO Z An Equine Veterinary Dictionary (new edition) *Peter Rossdale and Susan M. Wreford*
THE HORSE OWNER'S HANDBOOK *Monty Mortimer*
THE HORSE RIDER'S HANDBOOK *Monty Mortimer*
HUNTING An Introductory Handbook *R. W. F. Poole*
THE IMPERIAL HORSE The Saga of the Lipizzaners *Hans-Heinrich Isenbart and Emil Buhrer*
KEEPING A HORSE OUTDOORS *Susan McBane*
LUNGEING The Horse and Rider *Sheila Inderwick*
THE RIDING INSTRUCTOR'S HANDBOOK *Monty Mortimer*
RIDING AND STABLE SAFETY *Ann Brock*
TRANSPORTING YOUR HORSE OR PONY *Chris Larter and Tony Jackson*

A new series of practical and comprehensive equestrian books, written by acknowledged experts and illustrated throughout with specially commissioned photographs from top equestrian photographer Bob Langrish.

PRACTICAL DRESSAGE · Jane Kidd

Dressage is the fastest growing of all equestrian sports in Britain and the USA, and yet it remains shrouded in mystery. In this book Jane Kidd, a leading dressage writer and internationally successful competitor, has peeled away the layers of this mystery to present this fascinating discipline in a way that is at once clear, straightforward and practical.

The book treats dressage as the control and development of the horse's natural athleticism. The author begins by analysing the special talents needed by a dressage horse, and explains a number of techniques for maximising natural ability, both human and equine. She then moves on to examine the all-important – and often neglected – basic principles of dressage. With the help of over one hundred photographs, many in helpful sequences, plus detailed explanatory captions, the reader is guided through the various movements required in dressage tests up to advanced level, the training of the horse to fulfil these requirements, and finally the preparation for and riding of the test on the day.

This clearly written, well illustrated and entirely practical book will appeal to all those with an interest in dressage, and will enable riders, judges and spectators alike to appreciate and enjoy their sport to the full.

PRACTICAL SHOWING · Nigel Hollings

Nigel Hollings firmly believes that you never stop learning when producing horses and ponies for the show ring. During a career which began in childhood and spans over twenty years, he has collected a wealth of practical experience in the modern world of showing, and in this book he draws together the strands of that experience for the benefit of all those with an interest in the sport.

In his highly readable and original style, and with the help of many excellent photographs, Nigel Hollings guides the reader through the search for that elusive champion, and explains in detail how to school and prepare him or her for the show ring. It is this attention to the smallest detail, in everything from stable management to sewing in the last plait, that the author suggests is the key to success. Freely giving away his 'tricks of the trade' he discusses tack and turnout, and how to create the right 'picture' through a combination of ringcraft, showmanship and an understanding of what the judge will be looking for in the many different classes.

Like judging, the production of horses and ponies for the show ring is very much a matter of personal opinion, and it is on this basis that Nigel Hollings has produced this down-to-earth guide to showing. An essentially practical book which will prove an invaluable source of reference for both the novice and more experienced exhibitor, it is nevertheless stamped with a sense of humour – without which, the author suggests, you will not survive for long in the showing game!

PRACTICAL SHOWJUMPING · Peter Churchill

Peter Churchill has been involved in the business and observation of showjumping horses and riders for over thirty years, and in this book he draws on his wealth of experience to provide a practical guide for all those with a real interest in the sport.

The two essentials for success in the showjumping ring are the right attitude and the right horse, and the author takes a detailed look at both, before moving on to discuss the practical training of horse and rider. From basic principles, the reader is guided through a progressive programme of fitness, groundwork and training over fences, with the emphasis always firmly on the vital relationship between horse and rider. Equipment and training facilities, jumping practice and techniques are all covered, culminating in preparations for the show and how to ride the course itself.

Whether you are already training your horse for the showjumping ring or simply enjoy watching the experts in action, this practical book, written by one of our best known equestrian authors, will prove an invaluable addition to every showjumping enthusiast's bookshelf.

In preparation:
PRACTICAL EVENTING · Jane Holderness-Roddam
PRACTICAL HORSEMASTERSHIP · Susan McBane